W9-CLO-774

A SKETCH OF CHESTER HARDING, ARTIST

Drawn By His Own Hand

Library of American Art

A SKETCH OF
CHESTER HARDING, ARTIST

Drawn By His Own Hand

Edited by Margaret E. White

Annotations by W. P. G. Harding

Kennedy Galleries, Inc. • *Da Capo Press*
New York • *1970*

This edition of *A Sketch of Chester Harding, Artist* is an unabridged
republication of the revised edition published in
Boston and New York in 1929.

Library of Congress Catalog Card Number 70-87681

SBN 306-71711-5

Published by
Kennedy Galleries, Inc.
20 East 56th Street, New York, N.Y. 10022
and
Da Capo Press
A Division of Plenum Publishing Corporation
227 West 17th Street, New York, N.Y. 10011

Manufactured in the United States of America

A SKETCH OF
CHESTER HARDING, ARTIST

Chester Harding
Self-portrait, painted about 1860

A SKETCH OF
CHESTER HARDING, ARTIST

DRAWN BY HIS OWN HAND

EDITED BY HIS DAUGHTER
MARGARET E. WHITE

New Edition

WITH ANNOTATIONS BY HIS GRANDSON
W. P. G. HARDING

BOSTON AND NEW YORK
HOUGHTON MIFFLIN COMPANY
The Riverside Press Cambridge
1929

The Riverside Press
CAMBRIDGE · MASSACHUSETTS
PRINTED IN THE U.S.A.

CONTENTS

CONTENTS

CHAPTER VII

CHAPTER VIII. 1846–1847

CHAPTER IX. 1847–1866

ILLUSTRATIONS

ILLUSTRATIONS

INTRODUCTION TO NEW EDITION

WE are told in the Bible that, after creating the universe, God made man in his own image. In the field of art, there are many beautiful representations of scenes on land and sea which have brought fame to the artists who produced them; but in all ages a majority of the most noted artists have been those who painted the human face and form. Many an artist has enjoyed popularity and great reputation during his lifetime only to have his fame, after the sunset glow following death had faded away, more or less obscured for a period of years. But often there comes a time, some generations later, when public interest in his work revives, and the fame of the artist assumes again the brilliancy of bygone days. In the case of a portrait painter, this is due in part no doubt to the historic interest which attaches to the subjects of his portraits, but when the portraits are well executed and are accepted as accurate likenesses, this revival of interest extends to the artist himself.

In recent years, there has been a marked revival of interest in the paintings of Chester Harding, a self-made American artist who was at the height of his career one hundred years ago, and who died a year after the end of the Civil War. He was not of the early American era as were Copley, West, the elder Peale, Trumbull, and Stuart, but lived rather in a transition period, with the younger Peale, Allston, Inman, Morse, Elliot, and Sully as contemporaries. His span of life extended from 1792 to 1866. At the time of his birth, George Washington was serving his first term as President, and when he died, Andrew Johnson was in the White House. Mr. Harding began to paint portraits in Pittsburgh in 1818 when he was nearly twenty-six years of age, and his last portrait — of General Sherman — was painted forty-eight years later. During his long career he painted several thousand portraits. His fields of activity included Pittsburgh, Paris, Kentucky, St. Louis, Philadelphia, New Orleans, Washington, Baltimore, New York, Boston, London, Glasgow, and, at times between professional visits elsewhere, Springfield, Massachusetts, in which city he made his home for the last thirty-five years of his life. Among his American sitters were historic figures of Revolutionary times, and others prominent in civil and military life from the beginning of the nineteenth century down to the Civil War. He painted from life one or more portraits of Daniel Boone; Charles Carroll of Carrollton, signer of the Declaration of Independence; Chief Justice John Marshall; Presidents Madison, Monroe, and John Quincy Adams; William Wirt, Henry Clay, John C. Calhoun, John Randolph, Daniel Webster, Joseph

x

INTRODUCTION TO NEW EDITION

Story, William H. Seward, Edward Everett, Abbott Lawrence, Amos Lawrence, Henry W. Longfellow, Washington Irving, and General Sherman. He painted portraits of many celebrities in England such as the Duke of Sussex, son of George III, the Dukes of Gloucester, Norfolk, Hamilton, and Gordon, Mr. Coke of Holkham, Mr. Owen of New Lanark, Sir Archibald Alison the historian, Samuel Rogers the banker-poet, and Lord Aberdeen.

Mr. Harding's account of his life in England is most interesting, and one wonders how an American, with a background of only a few years in art, could have obtained so readily patrons of such high degree. He arrived in London August 23, 1823, and began his first portrait on September 2. On January 14, 1824, he began the portrait of H.R.H. the Duke of Sussex, which he finished on January 19. In Mr. Harding's diary he naïvely remarks that in England 'it is looked upon as a mark of great distinction to paint one of the royal family.' Six years before, the artist was painting signs in Pittsburgh. There is no evidence, however, that Mr. Harding's head was turned by the flattering attentions he received abroad. Naturally he was appreciative, but he was proud of his American birth and never attempted to conceal his Americanism. He made the personal acquaintance of Sir Thomas Lawrence and of other leading British artists, and derived much pleasure and profit from a study of their paintings. The effect of this contact is revealed in his own work. Before Mr. Harding went to England, his only training had been in the Philadelphia Academy, where he spent two months in making studies from paintings there. He saw there some of the works of Gilbert Stuart, whom he always regarded as 'the greatest portrait painter America has ever produced,' and thereafter, until he went abroad, his paintings, the heads especially, bore an impress of the Stuart influence. After his return in 1826, however, his portraits show very markedly the Lawrence influence.

Mr. Harding's portraits have, however, an individuality of their own, and, although seldom if ever signed, are readily identified by connoisseurs. His heads were generally carefully and subtly modeled, and give the impression of sureness and freedom in execution. He was a rapid worker, and frequently completed a portrait in five days. He was not always careful in his drawing, which he seemed to regard as mechanical, but almost invariably the artist caught the likeness and character of the subject so well that defective drawing and haste in finishing draperies and backgrounds are overlooked. Mr. Harding had a genius for color, and is regarded by many as one of the best colorists America has produced. Those of his paintings which have been carefully preserved, or which have been cleaned and restored, are much sought after for public museums and private collections. It is unfortunate that with few exceptions his best work is not represented in our museums.

The growing demand for good examples of the work of Chester Harding has led the writer to believe that art-lovers might like to know something of the artist — his grandfather.

In 1866, one of the daughters of the artist, Mrs. Margaret E. White, had published shortly after her father's death, for the family and friends, a sketch of his life, which was in part an autobiography. This little book was entitled 'My Egotistography.' In 1890, Mrs. White edited and published a larger edition of this, mainly for relatives, although a limited number of copies were made available for distribution to the public. This was at a time when the 'sunset glow' following the artist's death had passed, and before the historical perspective was strong enough to bring about a renaissance of his reputation. This book is now out of print and copies are hard to obtain, although dealers occasionally are able to furnish second-hand copies. Mrs. White, the last survivor of the nine children of Mr. Harding, died many years ago, but the writer has secured the permission of her daughter, Miss Eliza Orne White, and of the publishers, to incorporate in this volume the text of the edition of 1890 with such annotations as seemed to be advisable. There are inserted photogravures of a number of portraits by Mr. Harding which were painted in this country and in England at various periods. The selections have been made in some cases because of the historical interest attached to the subjects, and in others because of the merits of the portraits themselves.

W. P. G. HARDING

INTRODUCTION TO THE EDITION OF 1890

By Margaret E. White

THE generation to which Chester Harding belonged has passed off the stage. There must be many still living, however, who can recall him as an old man of commanding presence, with white hair and flowing beard, whose uncommonly tall figure, though slightly bowed by age, was still enough above the average height to make him conspicuous in any assembly; and whose handsome face expressed kindliness and humor. Nature was bountiful to him in an unusual degree, and to uncommon personal attractions added a mind of more than ordinary power, quick perceptions, and a love for the beautiful in nature and art. He was so ready to see and assimilate into his own being all the refinements of cultivated men and manners that, for those who saw him for the first time, it was difficult to believe that he was absolutely without school education, and that he had grown to maturity in the wilds of what was then the far West. Washington Allston, in a letter to a friend, writes of him:

In most cases we should regard as a misfortune the want of early education, which was denied Mr. Harding's youth, but Nature has been too liberal to him to make any feel, however his own modesty may cause him to regret, the need of it, for in forming him she has not only made him a painter, but a gentleman; and you know her too well not to know that she does her work far better than any Schools.[1]

His appearance in Boston, sixty years ago, was greeted with enthusiasm, and for the moment he was the paramount object of interest. It showed the quality of the man that the flattering attentions which he received did not in the least bias his judgment of his own worth, nor create a ripple of vanity in his breast.

He was an incessant worker. The needs of his large family gave him but small opportunity for leisure. He so deeply felt the deficiencies of his own mental training that he was eager to give to his children all the educational advantages that money could procure, and they were sent to the best schools of the period. To secure the funds necessary to meet these expenses required constant care and forethought, and obliged him to go from city to city to find the supply of sitters, which too long a stay in one place was sure to exhaust. This made his life a roving one, and kept him much from home. He was singularly fortunate, however, in his wife. Her uncommon powers of judgment, and her thoroughly well-balanced nature, made her an admirable counterpoise to his more impulsive temperament. His frequent and prolonged absences from home threw the chief care and responsibility of bringing up their ten children upon her. Towards the close of her life she writes, 'To-

[1] From *Lippincott's Magazine*, January, 1874, 'Chester Harding, the self-made Artist,' by Osmond Tiffany.

morrow I shall have been married twenty-four years, and my husband has not been at home for more than ten years of that time. The longest stay he has ever made without going away at all is one year.' She relieved her husband of most of the cares which commonly devolve upon the father of a family, and left him free to come and go as he thought best. After her unlooked-for and untimely death, at fifty, William B. O. Peabody, D.D., characterized her as 'wise, disinterested, true-hearted, of few words but strong affections — feeling that her many cares within the domestic circle did not allow her to wander often or far beyond it, and yet always earnest to do what she was able in the cause of humanity.'

Her friend, Mrs. A. J. Lyman, of Northampton, thus speaks of her in a letter to her sister:[1]

You have heard of the sudden death of Mrs. Harding? There has always been something about her that I have felt a great respect for; a quiet consistency in goodness, a common-sense purpose that attained its end, a cultivated perception of moral sentiment, as well as the beautiful in nature. And everything about her so unpretending and sincere that one could not know her well and withhold their respect. Contemplating her character strengthens my confidence in the goodness of human nature. It gives me faith in virtue, and makes me feel that it is a reality.

The death of such a woman was an irreparable loss to her husband and family.

[1] *Recollections of my Mother*, by Susan I. Lesley, p. 391.

INTRODUCTION TO THE EDITION OF 1890

Could a complete list of Mr. Harding's works be given, it would be a worthy monument to his industry. He worked rapidly, and his fine physical organization helped him to bear the strain of incessant application to his brush. He was rarely ill. He had occasional attacks of dyspepsia as well as painter's colic, but a few days or weeks of trout-fishing, for which he had a passion, or of hunting, would bring him right again.

Owing to his roving habits his portraits are scattered all over the Union, as well as through England and Scotland, which makes it impossible to get anything like a complete list of them. It is safe to say, however, that there are few of the eminent men of the United States who lived during the first thirty years of Mr. Harding's career whom he did not put on canvas. His likenesses, especially of men, were true and life-like. In a biographical notice of him in the 'Atlantic Monthly' for April, 1867, Samuel Bowles says of them:

A characteristic of his portraits was their suggestiveness. They seem to give us, not only the prominent expression of the countenance at the moment, but the possibilities of its expression in other moods. Hints of temperament and of character lurk in the fine lines which nature draws upon the living face; the more observable features really have but little part in the changing play of the countenance. And in Harding's portraits the chief excellence is their thorough comprehension of the subject, their representation of the man, and not simply of the conformation of his features at a particular period.

Among the many testimonials which the fidelity of

his likenesses was constantly receiving, none pleased Mr. Harding so much as the following:

A lady had recently died, and her pet cat had been wandering dejectedly about the house, evidently in search of something which she missed. At last she entered a room, where a likeness (by Harding) of her late mistress was standing on a sofa. The creature at once gave a bound, and tried to settle herself in her accustomed place on the old lady's lap.

Mr. Harding's personal appearance was very striking. A friend says of him, 'He was the finest specimen of manly beauty I ever saw.' In stature he was far above the average, measuring six feet three in his stockings; while his frame was so finely proportioned that his height was not fully appreciated until compared with that of an average-sized man. His muscular power was prodigious; and one of his brothers relates that, when he was eighteen years old, his feats of strength were the wonder of the neighborhood. While he was helping his father to clear up the land, after moving to western New York, he with the help of a friend, also of great size and strength, would themselves drag away and pile up the fallen timber, instead of resorting to the use of oxen, as their fellow-workmen were accustomed to do. In chopping wood, these two could each chop, split, and pile four cords of wood a day, which was just double the amount of an ordinary day's work.

His hands and feet were so large that he was obliged

to import his gloves, and to have his lasts made for him. The width between his eyes was such that an ordinary pair of spectacles would but half cover them. His uncommon size sometimes brought him into comically inconvenient situations. He used to tell with great glee, how, in warm weather, he would draw his short bedstead up to the window, in some out-of-the-way country tavern, and have the comfort of stretching himself at full length, by resting his feet on the window-sill. Once, in making a journey on a canal-boat, he found that he had not room to turn over in his berth; but as he was sadly cramped by lying on one side so long, he had to find relief, which he did by squeezing himself sideways between the berths and the table which extended down the cabin, until he reached the small vestibule on the outside of the boat. Here he had room to turn around, and when he reached his narrow bed again, he, of course, was able to get into it on his other side and to spend the remainder of the night in comparative comfort. During the later years of his life he wore a full beard, which as well as his hair was almost white, giving him a patriarchal appearance. A few months before his death, he sat to an artist as a model for the head of Saint Peter.

There was in his manner, particularly to young people, a heartiness and kindliness which universally attracted them to him; and he possessed an intuitive perception of other people's tastes and feelings which

xx

prevented his saying or doing anything that would be disagreeable to them. He was full of humor, and had a thorough appreciation of wit in others.

This quality often stood him in stead of any more serious way of criticising the faults of his family. One of his sons, whose usual demeanor was so staid that he was nicknamed the Deacon, had been sent from college to spend a few weeks in the bosom of his family, for blowing tin horns on the night of April first. The ludicrousness of the whole proceeding entertained the young man's father greatly, and no other notice was ever taken of the misdemeanor than a reference to him, when a question about any literary matter came up in the family, saying, 'There is my son who has just graduated with college honors: ask him, he can undoubtedly tell us.'

He had a unique way of expressing his hearer's quickness to appreciate his jokes, by a series of telegraphic signs made to one of his children. If his hearer was slow of comprehension he formed an obtuse angle with his fingers; if the reverse, an acute one, and no one but the favored child had any idea of his opinion having been given.

He had a quick, impulsive nature; and, after once coming to a decision about any course of action, was very eager to carry out his plans. His wife was fond of giving an account of their wedding, as an illustration of this trait.

The wedding-day had been fixed for February 15, 1815, and on the preceding day the bride was making her last preparations for the great event. The guests had been invited: the wedding-cake was in the oven; and her brother had been dispatched to a neighboring town for the white kid gloves and sash. Presently the bridegroom-elect drove up to the door in a sleigh, and, after the first salutations had passed, announced that he had come to be married on *that* day; for the snow was melting so fast that, if they waited twenty-four hours, they could not get back to Caledonia. So they were married the day beforehand. 'And,' his wife was accustomed to say, 'it has been the day beforehand ever since.'

He was a good son and brother; and, as soon as his own circumstances warranted it, he not only extended pecuniary aid to his father and mother, but interested himself in the education of those members of the family younger than himself, whom he endeavored to incite to a desire for intellectual improvement, and which he gave them opportunities to attain.

He had a sunny temper, which, combined with his confidence in his own power of overcoming obstacles, made him meet the little irritations of life either with a laugh and jest, or at most with a quick, impatient 'Pshaw!' which seemed to be all the outlet his disturbed feelings needed. He had quick inventive powers, and the mechanical skill to carry out his ideas: so that he never seemed at fault in any emergency, but always had some way of getting out of every difficulty; which, combined with his uncommon strength, gave those who were dependent upon him an unusual feeling of reliance and trust.

His love for music amounted to a passion; and his correctness of ear was such that he became an accomplished performer on the clarinet, without knowing how to read a note of music. Any air that he could sing he could play at once upon the piano, without striking a false note; and he whistled finely.

His love of nature was very noticeable; and he seemed to possess peculiar power over her, by which he could make her subservient to his wishes. Every living thing that his hands touched was sure to flourish; and it used to be a saying in the family that, if 'father were to plant a brick, it would come up a tree.' When he was preparing to build his house on Chestnut Street, in Springfield, he wished to make an artificial pond on his grounds. To do this, it was necessary to move some well-grown trees, with trunks as large as a man's leg. It was in the month of August, when, of course, they were in full leaf. He had them carried some feet, reset them; and, in spite of the prophecies to the contrary of all his neighbors, they not only lived, but were uninjured by their little midsummer excursion.

Landscape gardening was his delight, and perhaps he did more to give an impulse to the taste which is now so conspicuous in the well-arranged and beautifully adorned grounds about the dwelling-houses in Springfield than any other one person. He was closely associated with the late W. B. O. Peabody, D.D., in laying out the grounds of the beautiful Springfield Cemetery; and the arrangement of the water-works was entirely his own. He spent days there, directing the workmen, and often using the spade himself. The pines that stand at the entrance, now grown into large trees, were set with his own hands.

In the following pages, Mr. Harding tells his own story. The narrative was prepared for his children, and, immediately after his death, was printed by them and privately circulated among his many friends. It was very warmly received, and the notices of it in private letters or in the public prints were numerous and eulogistic. To this have been added extracts from letters which came into the editor's possession after 'My Egotistography'[1] was printed.

The story of a life of such perseverance under difficulties, such unflagging industry, such devotion to a worthy aim, and a picture of such simplicity and poise of character, cannot but be helpful to the young who, like him, have their own fortunes to make in the world. If it shall help one such to a faithful use of the talents given him, looking only to the attainment of his best ideal for his reward, this story will not have been written in vain.

[1] This was the name Mr. Harding playfully gave to the autobiographical sketch, which he felt was too slight to pretend to any more assuming title.

A SKETCH OF
CHESTER HARDING, ARTIST

THE FORBEARS OF CHESTER HARDING

The Harding family came to Massachusetts from England in the year 1623.

1. ABRAHAM HARDING, recorded as an inhabitant of Dedham, Massachusetts, in 1638. Married Elizabeth Harding who came from England. Removed to Braintree in 1642. Died suddenly March 22, 1655, being then 40 years old. Had built a costly house for the times. Was a glover and leather dresser.

2. ABRAHAM HARDING, posthumous son of above, was born August 12 or 18, 1655, at Medfield. Was a man of character and consideration — Selectman, moderator, etc. Married first Mary Mason and next, Sarah Fairbank, daughter of John Merrifield. Died in 1734.

3. SAMUEL HARDING, son of above, born in 1700, died 1780. Married Mary Cutler at Boston, 1722, who died in 1778, aged 78. Owned a slave, Dinah.

4. SAMUEL HARDING, son of above, born January 7, 1726-27. Married Abigail Fisher, October 24, 1748. Settled in Woodstock, Connecticut. In 1775 moved to Deerfield, Massachusetts. Had twin sons, Abiel and Abijah. Died in 1800 leaving a good estate.

5. ABIEL HARDING, son of above, born 1756. Married Olive Smith of Whately, Mass. Resided in Conway and Hatfield and in 1806 moved to Sullivan County, New York. Died at Barre, New York, in 1849. Had eleven children who lived to maturity and three who died in infancy. When 92 years old he walked 15 miles to visit a daughter and walked back the next day. Was a revolutionary pensioner and had fought in the Indian wars previously. Was at Bennington, Stony Point, Yorktown, and other battles.

A SKETCH OF
CHESTER HARDING, ARTIST

• •

PREFACE TO 'MY EGOTISTOGRAPHY'

I HAVE often been importuned by my children and numerous friends to write a history of my life, which, perhaps, has been more varied and eventful than common. This I have endeavored to do; and, if the perusal of this imperfect sketch shall give them pleasure, I shall be amply repaid for the labor the work has cost me.

I trust that some of my young readers may find encouragement in the difficulties I have overcome, and the success which has followed my perseverance.

CHESTER HARDING

SPRINGFIELD, *June*, 1865

CHAPTER I

OF my ancestors I know nothing beyond my grandparents. My paternal grandfather was a substantial farmer in Deerfield, Massachusetts. He lived in a two-story house, which to my youthful imagination was a palace; filled many offices of profit and trust in the town, lived to a good old age, and was gathered to his fathers with the universal respect of his neighbors.

On the maternal side, I can go no farther back. My grandfather Smith was a farmer, who lived to a ripe old age, and died much respected. For many years he held

3

the office of deacon in the town of Whately, where he resided. I was born in the adjoining town of Conway, on the 1st of September, 1792.

My parents were poor; and, of course, I was brought up like all other poor children of that period. My first recollection is of our moving from Conway to Hatfield. I well remember the brook that ran close by the house we lived in there, and the amusement I had in catching the little fishes with a pinhook. As I grew older, I began to fish with a real hook, and to catch trout. Like most boys of my age I thought more of 'going a-fishing' than of all other indulgences. Indeed it amounted almost to a passion with me. I would go miles on an errand, or do any amount of service, for a penny or two, that I might be able to buy my fishhooks.

From the age of eight to ten, I lived in Bernardston, with an aunt. Here again I had a brook that constantly enticed me from my daily duties, which consisted chiefly of the care of a flock of young geese. I played truant nearly every day, and as often was whipped by my aunt. I returned home at the end of two years. We were very poor, and were often in need of the necessaries of life. My father was a good man, of unexceptionable habits; but he was not thrifty, and did little towards the support of the family. He had a great inventive genius, and turned all his powers towards the discovery of perpetual motion. At the time of his death his attic was full of machines, the making of which had occupied a large

4

part of his life. But this brought no bread and butter to his hungry children.

One hard winter he went to Northfield, Massachusetts, to get work, where my mother supposed he was earning something for the maintenance of the family. While there, he had the small-pox; and all the work he did was to make the body of a very large bass-viol. Imagine the disappointment of his family when they found that this monster skeleton was all he had brought home to them!

My mother was a noble woman. In all the trials of poverty, she managed to keep her children decently dressed, that they might go to meeting on Sunday, and make a respectable appearance among other boys. It is true our more prosperous cousins rather turned up their noses at us now and then, much to our mortification.

At the age of twelve, I was hired out at six dollars a month to a Mr. Graves, in Hatfield. He was a good and religious man. I lived with him two years. I went to school in the winter, and learned enough to read the Bible. I partook largely of the religious sentiment that pervaded the family. I said my prayers night and morning, and was deemed a model boy. At the age of fourteen, my father moved to the western part of New York State, into Madison County,[1] then an unbroken wilderness. Now began my hard work and harder fare. Our first business was to build a log house, and to clear a patch of ground, and fit it for seed. I had two brothers

[1] Monroe County.

older than myself, the oldest of whom was a chair-maker by trade, and made common flag-bottomed chairs for the neighbors. By this means we could get an occasional piece of pork, some flour and potatoes; whilst my father and his other boys wielded the axe — that great civilizer.

We finished the house, and in the spring we had a few acres felled and ready for burning. We planted corn and potatoes amongst the blackened stumps; fortunately, the crop needed no labor beyond that of planting. Before the season was far spent, we were all down with chills and fever. We managed somehow to live through that year, which was the hardest we had ever seen. I grew strong, and was distinguished for my skill in using the axe. I could lift a larger log than any one else, and, in short, at eighteen was considered a prodigy of strength. Our means for intellectual development were very scant. Our parents would sometimes read the Bible to us, the only book we had in the house; and occasionally we were blessed with a visit from some itinerant preacher, when the whole forest settlement would meet in some large building, either the school-house or a barn, and listen to his divine teachings. At nineteen I changed my mode of life. I began to think there might be an easier way of getting a living than by cutting down and clearing up the heavily timbered forest, and worked one winter with my brother at turning stuff for chairs.

About this time war was declared between the United States and Great Britain. A military spirit was aroused throughout the whole of western New York, and I imbibed as much of it as any one. I had become a distinguished drummer, and had drummed for pay, until I was obliged to do military duty. My brother, next younger than myself, was one of the first to enlist in the service for one year. The troops were soon called to active service at Oswego. After six months he was anxious to return home. I offered myself, and was accepted as a substitute. As he was a drummer, I could easily fill his place.

Nothing of importance broke in upon the monotony of camp-life until mid-winter, when we were ordered to prepare three days' provisions, and to march next morning for Sacket's Harbor. The snow was very deep, and the weather cold; yet the days of our march were holidays, when compared to camp-life. We committed many depredations on our way, such as stealing chickens, or, on rare occasions, a pig. I was on the rear section of the column one day, and with another soldier had fallen so far behind that we had lost sight of the troops. Being uncertain which of two roads to take, we applied at a house which was near, for directions. 'Oh!' said the woman, 'you have only to follow the feathers.'

Sacket's Harbor was threatened with an attack by the British. They had a considerable force in Canada, nearly opposite; and the lake at that point was completely frozen over. We were constantly drilled, and kept in readiness for an attack. We had several alarms, and were often drummed out at midnight to face the foe; but he was only found in the imagination of the frightened sentinel.

Sickness now began to thin our ranks. Every hour in the day some poor fellow would be followed to Briarfield; and the tune, 'Away goes the merryman home to his grave,' played on returning from the burial, was too often heard to leave the listeners indifferent to its notes. My turn came at last, and I was taken down with the prevailing disease, dysentery; but my lieutenant took me to his own quarters, instead of sending me to the hospital. He was my neighbor, and in this instance proved himself to be one in the Scripture sense. Had I gone to the hospital I should probably have shared the fate of nearly all who went there, and have been carried to Briarfield. As soon as I recovered sufficient strength to get home, I was discharged, as my time of service was nearly up.

I suffered intensely on my way home. I was thinly clad, without overcoat or gloves. I started from camp with a lad who was taking back a horse that an officer had ridden to Sacket's Harbor: he was warmly clothed and of a very robust make. We traveled on, until I began to feel a good deal fatigued. We at last came to a house where we had been told we could find accommodation. We arrived there just at dusk, and, to our dismay, were told by the master of the house, that he could not keep us, and that he had nothing on hand for either man or beast to eat. It was six miles to the next house and the road lay on the beach of the lake, exposed to the piercing winds which blew over it. We started off, I on foot as before, while the boy was mounted. I had to run to keep warm. At length we came in sight of a light; but what was our dismay to find an open river between us and it! I shouted to the utmost capacity of my lungs, but could get no response. What was to be done? Nothing, but to return to the shelter we had left an hour and a half before. I started back at the same speed I came; but, before we had gone half the distance, my strength gave out, leaving me no other alternative but to mount the horse with the boy. I soon found myself getting very cold, and a strong desire to go to sleep came over me. I looked at the thick clumps of evergreen that stood by our path, and thought seriously of lying down under one of them to wait until daylight. The boy was crying, and begged me to keep on, saying, 'If you lie down there, you will freeze to death,' which would indeed have been inevitable. I yielded to his entreaties, and we finally reached the house we had left three hours before. The boy was not much frozen, but I was badly bitten. My face, hands, and thighs were stiff. After a good deal of rapping and hallooing, the door was opened. The man of the house had been used to such scenes, and knew well what to do. He put my feet into cold water, at the same time making applications to my face, ears, and

9

legs. Mortal never suffered more acute pain than I did through that sleepless night. I experienced the truth of our host's statement with regard to provisions. The next day at noon, we started again on our perilous journey, having been assured that we were mistaken about the river being open. Traveling more leisurely than we had done the previous night, we reached the river again; and, owing to the intense cold, it was covered with a thin coat of ice, but not thick enough to bear a man in an upright position. I got a long pole, and, by putting myself in a swimming posture, reached the opposite shore in safety, though it was frightful to feel the ice, not much thicker than a pane of window-glass, bending under me. At the house I was told that the crossing was half a mile back. I recrossed the river; and, retracing our steps a mile, we found a blind road leading over the bluff, which soon took us in safety to a comfortable house, where we found enough to eat for ourselves and our horse. The next day I started for my home, where my sufferings were soon forgotten. I speedily recovered, and went to work with my brother. We had a contract for drum-making from the United States, which gave us employment all the following summer.

Early in the fall of this year I embarked in a new business. A mechanic had invented and patented a spinning-head, which was thought to be a great improvement upon the old plan. I accepted an offer he made me to sell the patent in the State of Connecticut.

CHESTER HARDING

The only thing in the way of my making a fortune was the want of capital. However, 'Where there's a will, there's a way.' I soon contrived to get a horse and wagon, and five or six dollars in money, besides a quantity of essences, such as peppermint, tansy, wintergreen, etc. With this fit-out I launched forth into the wide world in pursuit of fortune. There is no period in the history of a young man which awakens so many of the finer feelings of his nature as that when he leaves his home, and for the first time assumes the position and responsibility of an independent man. All the joyful recollections of that home he is about to leave, no matter how humble it is, rush with overwhelming force upon his susceptible heart. I started with all the firmness and resolution I could call to my aid; yet if my mother could have looked into my eyes, she would have seen them filled with big tears. I jumped into my wagon, whipped up my horse, and was soon out of sight of what, at that moment, seemed all the world to me.

I managed, in view of my small stock of money, to get along without drawing largely upon it. I often bartered my essences for a night's entertainment, and was going on swimmingly, until I came to a small town on the banks of the Mohawk. I stopped to bait my horse; and, as I was about to start, a man with a bundle of clothing in his hand wanted to get a ride as far as the next town, for which he would give me twenty-five cents. I, of course, was glad to avail myself of his offer. We had traveled perhaps a mile, when we over-took two men by the roadside, in violent dispute about a pack of cards. One was very drunk. My new friend proposed that we should stop and inquire into the rights of the case: so I pulled up. The drunken man was contending that he had won a quarter of a dollar of the other; whereupon he proceeded to show us how it was done. He had bet that the top card was the jack of clubs, and was willing to bet again that the top card was the jack of clubs; at the same time showing, as if by accident, that it was on the bottom of the pack. My friend bet him a quarter that it was not on the top, and won. He fixed his cards again very clumsily, as he was very drunk. I bet, and won. I bet a half next time; so did my friend: we lost. We now accused him of having two jacks in the pack, and my friend examined the pack, but found only one; and that he managed to drop into the bottom of the wagon, and covered it with his foot. The cards were again shuffled. We had no scruples about betting on a certainty, as it was to get our money back, so we each bet a dollar, but lost. In some mys-terious manner the card had been taken from under the foot. There was nothing to be done but to bear this loss as well as I could; and we started on, very sad. My companion had lost every cent he had in the world. He had a loaded whip, worth two or three dollars, that he urged me to buy. In pity for the poor fellow I gave him his price, when he suddenly recollected that he had left something at the tavern, and must go back. He soon overtook the two worthies we had just left, and all three joined in a hearty laugh. My eyes were instantly opened. I clenched my new whip, determined to go back and thrash the scoundrels; but as they were three to one, I finally thought better of it. I firmly believe that, if I had gone back, I should have killed one of them at least with my loaded whip. I traveled on, not much in love with myself. I bore the loss of the money better than I did the way in which it was lost. This lesson has never been forgotten. I finally reached Connecticut, the field of my future operations. I returned with more money than I started with, and had a surplus of fifty or sixty wooden clocks and several watches, which I had taken for the patent in different parts of the State.

Near the close of the war, my brother (younger than myself) and I went into the cabinet and chair manufactory in Caledonia, a small town in Livingston County, New York.

At this juncture [1816] I happened to meet with Caroline Woodruff, a lovely girl of twenty, with handsome, dark eyes, fine brunette complexion, and of an amiable disposition. I fell in love with her at first sight. I can remember the dress she wore at our first meeting as well as I do those beautiful eyes. It was a dark crimson, woolen dress, with a neat little frill about the neck. I saw but little of her, for her family soon moved to a distance, forty or fifty miles. Though she was absent, however, her image was implanted too deeply in my heart to be forgotten. It haunted me day and night. At length I took the resolution to go to see her; which was at once carried out. I set out on foot, found her, and proposed, and was bid to wait a while for my answer. I went again, in the same way, and this time had the happiness to be accepted; and, three weeks after, she became my wife, and accompanied me to my home. We had hardly reached it before I was sued for a small debt, which I could not meet: in short, business was not very flourishing, and we were much embarrassed.

To relieve myself I went into an entirely new business — that of tavern-keeping. Here I paid off some old debts by making new ones. Matters, however, did not improve: on the contrary, creditors grew more clamorous and threatening. Nothing could strike me with more horror than the thought of being shut up in Batavia jail. At that time the barbarous practice of imprisonment for debt was in full force. My mind was made up. On Saturday night I took leave of my wife and child, and left for the headwaters of the Allegheny River. As soon as the river opened I took passage on a raft, and worked my way down to Pittsburgh. Here I was at a loss what to do. Times were hard; and, besides, I was not a good enough mechanic to get employment at the only trade I knew anything of. I finally got a job at

14

Mrs. Chester Harding

house painting; but I felt lonely and unhappy. As soon as I had saved a few dollars I started for my wife and child. I walked over mountains and through wild forests, with no guide but the blazed trees. Bears, wolves, deer, and turkeys I met so often that I would hardly turn around to look at them. At last I reached the settlement within a few miles of Caledonia. Here I halted till night, thinking it safer to travel by moonlight than in broad day. As it grew dark I started, tired and foot-sore. I saw a horse grazing in the road, and the thought struck me that he could ease my weary limbs. I succeeded in catching and mounting him; and, by means of my staff or walking-stick, I steered him to the street of Caledonia. I then turned him on his way home, and bade him good-night. I remained in close concealment three or four days, and, when all was ready, started again for the headwaters of the Allegheny, but not alone: this time my wife and child were with me. We experienced many hardships on our way, but nothing of particular interest occurred. At Oleans Point we embarked upon a raft, with a comfortable shanty on board, and in a week floated down the river to Pittsburgh. Before I had left Pittsburgh, I had rented a ten-footer, with two rooms in it; so we went directly there. All our availables consisted of one bed, and a chest of clothing, and some cooking utensils, so that we had little labor in getting settled down.

But now all my money was gone, and how to get more

15

was the question. I could find no work as a house painter, and what to do I did not know. I would walk about the town, and return to find my wife in tears — though she always had a smile for me. I went into the market the next morning, though for what purpose I could hardly tell, for I had not one cent of money. At last I ventured to ask the price of a beefsteak. I had the impudence to say to the man that I should like that piece very much, but that I had no change with me. To my great surprise he said I could take it, and pay for it the next time I came. As I had made the acquaintance of Mr. Sands, a barber who occupied the twin part of the house I was in, I went to his wife, and asked her to loan me half a loaf of bread, which she did cheerfully. If we went hungry that day it was not because we had not enough to eat, and that, too, with an honest appetite.

There was an opening just now for a sign painter. I had talked with Neighbor Sands upon the subject of my becoming one. He approved the plan, and was the means of my getting an order. A Mr. W. H. Wetherell wanted a sign painted in gold letters on both sides, so as to project it into the street. I agreed to do it; but where was the stock of gold paint and board to come from? I went into Neighbor Sands' half a dozen times for the purpose of asking him to lend me the money to procure the materials, and as often my heart failed me. At last I made a grand effort, and said, 'Neighbor Sands,

16

CHESTER HARDING

I wish you would lend me twenty dollars for a few days, as I have no money by me that is current.' 'Certainly, with pleasure.' I could hardly believe it real. I took the money, and hurried into my room, and threw it into my wife's lap. She was frightened, fearing I had obtained it by some unlawful means. The first use I made of it was to go to the market, to pay the credulous butcher; and to buy some vegetables, tea, sugar, and some other little luxuries. I got my sign-board made, bought my gold leaf, paints, etc.; went to a printer, and got some very large impressions of the alphabet; and, having in my chair-making experience learned the art of gilding, I soon had my sign finished, and paid back my neighbor his money. He never knew that I was not flush of money; but his kindness I never forgot. I was at once established as a sign painter, and followed that trade for a year.

CHAPTER II

About this time [1818] I fell in with a portrait painter by the name of Nelson — one of the primitive sort. He was a sign, ornamental, and portrait painter. He had for his sign a copy of the 'Infant Artists' of Sir Joshua Reynolds, with this inscription, 'Sign, Ornamental, and Portrait Painting executed on the shortest notice, with neatness and dispatch.' It was in his sanctum that I first conceived the idea of painting heads. I saw his portraits, and was enamored at once. I got him to paint me and my wife, and thought the pictures perfection. He would not let me see him paint, nor would he give me the least idea how the thing was done. I took the pictures home, and pondered on them, and wondered how it was possible for a man to produce such wonders of art. At length my admiration began to yield to an ambition to do the same thing. I thought of it by day, and dreamed of it by night, until I was stimulated to make an attempt at painting myself. I got a board; and, with such colors as I had for use in my trade, I began a portrait of my wife. I made a thing that looked like her. The moment I saw the likeness I became frantic with delight: it was like the discovery of a new sense; I could think of nothing else. From that time sign painting became odious, and was much neglected.

18

I next painted a razeed portrait of an Englishman who was a journeyman baker, for which I received five dollars. He sent it to his mother in London. I also painted portraits of the man and his wife with whom I boarded, and for which I received, on account, twelve dollars each. This was in the winter season: the river was closed, and there was but little to be done in sign painting.

I shall always remember the friendship of an Irish apothecary, who, at this period of my history, encouraged me in my attempts at portrait painting, and allowed me to buy any material I needed, on credit, from his paint and drug store. I had been painting a second picture of my wife, and asked Nelson the painter to come and see it. He declared it to be no more like my wife than like him, and said further that it was utter nonsense for me to try to paint portraits at my time of life: he had been ten years in learning the trade. To receive such a lecture, and such utter condemnation of my work, when I expected encouragement and approval, was truly disheartening. He left me; and I was still sitting before the picture, in great dejection, when my friend the doctor came in. He instantly exclaimed, with much apparent delight, 'That's good; first-rate, a capital likeness,' etc. I then repeated what Nelson had just said. He replied that it was sheer envy; that he never painted half so good a head, and never would. The tide of hope began to flow again, and I grew more

19

and more fond of head painting. I now regarded sign painting merely as a necessity, while my whole soul was wrapped up in my new love, and I neglected my trade so much that I was kept pretty short of money. I resorted to every means to eke out a living. I sometimes played the clarionet for a tight-rope dancer, and on market-days would play at the window of the museum to attract the crowd to the exhibition. For each of these performances I would get a dollar.

I was strictly temperate in my habits, and seldom spent a sixpence for anything that we did not actually need; but I remember one occasion when my love for music and excitement got the better of my prudence. I had gone out one evening to borrow a dollar to go to market with the next morning, when, as I was sauntering about, I heard music, which attracted me to the spot. It was the performance of the orchestra of the theatre. It was a temporary building, loosely boarded; and as I looked through the cracks of the covering, I saw such a sight as I had never dreamed of. I went instantly to the door, got a ticket, and crowded my way in. By degrees I managed to get into a box which was full. I stood for the first hour in perfect amazement at the lords and ladies, and was overwhelmed by the brilliant lights and heavenly music. At the end of one of the acts one of the gentlemen left his seat, and went out; and I took it. He came back and claimed his seat. I was not inclined to admit his claim. I had paid my dollar, and told him I thought I had as good a right to a seat as he had; and that he could as well stand an hour as I. He prepared to eject me by force; but, as I unfolded my dimensions, he relinquished his purpose, and bore the loss of his seat as well as he could. I did not leave the theatre until the last lamp was extinguished. The play which had so enchanted me was Scott's 'Lady of the Lake.' This was my first acquaintance with the stage. I do not remember how we fared the next day in our marketing, but I presume I borrowed another dollar in the morning.

Up to this time I had never read any book but the Bible, and could only read that with difficulty. My wife, who had received a comparatively good education, and had once taught school, borrowed of one of the neighbors 'The Children of the Abbey,' a popular novel of that day. I was rather opposed to her reading it, as I had been taught to believe by my mother that cards and novels were the chief instruments of the Devil in seducing mortals from the paths of virtue. However, her desire to read it was too strong to be overcome by any objections I could raise, so I had to yield; but I insisted upon her reading it aloud. One dark and rainy day she commenced the reading. She read on till bedtime, and then proposed to leave the rest of the story until the next day; but I was altogether too eager to hear how the next chapter ended to consent to that. She was persuaded to read the next chapter, and the

next, and the next. In short, I kept her reading all
night, and gave her no rest until the novel was finished.
The first novel I ever read myself was 'Rob Roy.' I
could only read it understandingly by reading it aloud,
and to this day I often find myself whispering the words
in the daily newspaper.

My brother Horace, the chair-maker, was established
in Paris, Kentucky. He wrote to me that he was painting
portraits, and that there was a painter in Lexington who
was receiving fifty dollars a head. This price seemed
fabulous to me; but I began to think seriously of trying
my fortune in Kentucky. I soon settled upon the idea,
and acted at once.

Winding up my affairs in Pittsburgh, I found that
I had just money enough to take me down the river. I
knew a barber, by the name of Jarvis, who was going to
Lexington, and I proposed to join him in the purchase
of a large skiff. He agreed to it; and we fitted it up with
a sort of awning or tent, and embarked, with our wives
and children. Sometimes we rowed our craft; but of-
tener we let her float as she pleased, while we gave
ourselves up to music. He, as well as I, played the
clarionet; and we had much enjoyment on our voyage.
We arrived in Paris with funds rather low, but, as my
brother was well known there, I found no difficulty on
that score.[1]

[1] Mrs. Harding used to describe to her children how, when night fell, the
flatboat was moored to the shore, while the two families would find shelter

Here I began my career as a professional artist. I took a room, and painted the portrait of a very popular young man, and made a decided hit. In six months from that time, I had painted nearly one hundred portraits, at twenty-five dollars a head. The first twenty-five I took rather disturbed the equanimity of my conscience. It did not seem to me that the portrait was intrinsically worth that money; now, I know it was not.

I have stated previously that I was strictly temperate. This was not from principle, but simply because I did not want any stimulant. During my stay in Paris, I was constantly thrown into the society of those who did drink. It was the almost universal custom to take a julep before breakfast; and by degrees I fell into the habit of taking *my* julep, and sometimes two. I soon guessed where this would end, for I found that I felt uncomfortable unless I had my morning dram. I stopped short at once, and for five years never tasted a drop of ardent spirits. I was sometimes obliged to sip a glass of wine at the dinner-table.

Here it was that I mingled for the first time with the tip-top of society. I went at once, on my arrival in the town, to the first-class hotel. I found unspeakable embarrassment at the table, with so many fine young

in some Indian wigwam, sleeping on the floor with their feet towards the fire which was burning in the middle of the circle thus formed. The smoke found its way out of an opening left in the roof. The provisions of the party became nearly exhausted before they reached civilization, and she shared her last loaf of bread with her fellow-travelers, not knowing where the next mouthful was to come from for herself or child.

23

gentlemen, all so elegantly dressed, with ruffled shirts, rings on their white and delicate fingers, and diamond pins in their bosoms. They, no doubt, thought me very clownish, as I undoubtedly was. I found little respect paid me by them, until I began to attract the attention of their masters. I soon became a sort of lion, and grew very popular among these clerks, especially after I was so far advanced in the ways of society as to take my morning juleps.

Up to this time I had thought little of the profession, so far as its honors were concerned. Indeed, it had never occurred to me that it was more honorable or profitable than sign painting. I now began to entertain more elevated ideas of the art, and to desire some means of improvement. Finding myself in funds sufficient to visit Philadelphia, I did so, and spent two months in that city, devoting my time entirely to drawing in the Academy, and studying the best pictures, practicing at the same time with the brush. I would sometimes feel a good deal discouraged as I looked at the works of older artists. I saw the labor it would cost me to emulate them, working, as I should, under great disadvantages. Then again, when I had painted a picture successfully, my spirits would rise, and I would resolve that I could and would overcome every obstacle. One good effect of my visit to Philadelphia was to open my eyes to the merits of the works of other artists, though it took away much of my self-satisfaction. My own pictures did not look as well to my own eye as they did before I left Paris. I had thought then that my pictures were far ahead of Mr. Jewitt's, the painter my brother had written me about, who received such unheard-of prices, and who really was a good artist. My estimation of them was very different now: I found they were so superior to mine that their excellence had been beyond my capacity of appreciation.

When I returned to Kentucky [in 1820] I found that the scarcity of money, from which the State was then suffering, seriously affected my business; and after struggling on for a few months, without bettering my finances, I concluded to try a new field. I first tried my fortune in Cincinnati; but after waiting a week or two in vain for orders, I gave up all hope of succeeding there, and determined to push on to St. Louis. But how to get there was a puzzling question. I had used up all my money; but, in my palmy days in Paris, I had bought a dozen silver spoons, and a gold watch and chain for my wife. There was no way left for me now but to dispose of these superfluities. I went with them to a broker, and pawned them for money enough to take me and my family to Missouri. I had letters of introduction to St. Louis, and set off at once for that far-off city. We went as far as Louisville on a flatboat, and there found a steamboat ready to take passengers; and in ten days we were safely landed in St. Louis. I presented one of my letters to Governor Clarke, who was then Governor of the Territory, Indian Agent, etc., and he kindly helped me about getting a suitable room for a studio, and then offered himself as a sitter. This was an auspicious and cheering beginning. I was decidedly happy in my likeness of him, and, long before I had finished his head, I had others engaged; and for fifteen months I was kept constantly at work.

In June of this year I made a trip of one hundred miles for the purpose of painting the portrait of old Colonel Daniel Boone. I had much trouble in finding him. He was living, some miles from the main road, in one of the cabins of an old block-house which was built for the protection of the settlers against the incursions of the Indians. I found that the nearer I got to his dwelling, the less was known of him. When within two miles of his house, I asked a man to tell me where Colonel Boone lived. He said he did not know any such man. 'Why, yes, you do,' said his wife. 'It is that white-headed old man who lives on the bottom, near the river.' A good illustration of the proverb, that a prophet is not without honor save in his own country.

I found the object of my search engaged in cooking his dinner. He was lying in his bunk, near the fire, and had a long strip of venison wound around his ramrod, and was busy turning it before a brisk blaze, and using salt and pepper to season his meat. I at once told him the object of my visit. I found that he hardly knew what I meant. I explained the matter to him, and he

26

Daniel Boone
Painted in 1820

agreed to sit. He was ninety years old, and rather infirm; his memory of passing events was much impaired, yet he would amuse me every day by his anecdotes of his earlier life. I asked him one day, just after his description of one of his long hunts, if he never got lost, having no compass. 'No,' said he, 'I can't say as ever I was lost, but I was *bewildered* once for three days.'

He was much astonished at seeing the likeness. He had a very large progeny; one granddaughter had eighteen children, all at home near the old man's cabin: *they* were even more astonished at the picture than the old man himself.

I will mention in this connection the fact of my painting one of the Osage chiefs. There was a deputation from this tribe on a visit to Governor Clarke. I asked some of them to go to my room, and there showed them the portrait of Governor Clarke, at the sight of which they gave several significant grunts. They were not satisfied with merely looking, but went close to the picture, rubbed their fingers across the face, looked behind it, and showed great wonder. The old chief was a fine-looking man, of great dignity of manner. I asked him to sit for his portrait. He did so; and, after giving evident signs of pleasure at seeing himself reproduced on canvas, he said that I was a god (a great spirit), and if I would go home with him, I should be a brave, and have two wives.

27

The deputation went to Washington, where they stayed long enough to lose much, I may say nearly all, of that which ennobles the Indian character. I saw them on their return to St. Louis. They wore, instead of their own graceful blankets, a military dress with tawdry cotton epaulettes and cotton lace; and withal had fallen into the habit of getting beastly drunk. All the interest I had felt in them was gone.

The city became very sickly, and the weather was intensely hot. I decided to leave the city for a month or two. I hired a pair of horses and a close carriage and driver, and started for the town of Franklin, about two hundred miles from St. Louis, situated on the Missouri River. The day after we started I was taken violently ill of dysentery, and was reduced in one week to a skeleton.

We met with an adventure on our way, which I relate for the amusement of the younger portion of my readers. We stopped one day about noon to bait our horses. While waiting at the tavern, I saw the fresh skin of some wild animal, and inquired what it was. I was told that it was the skin of a panther that had been shot the night before, and that her mate was prowling about the prairie. The two had done great damage to the young cattle and hogs, and a deadly war had been waged against them. The whole settlement had turned out on the hunt, and at last had succeeded in killing one. We started to cross the prairie called the Twenty-Mile

Prairie, and traveled on through intense heat and swarms of flies until near night, and were within a mile of the wooded border, when the driver suddenly stopped, and called out, 'My God! massa, what dat dar?' I lifted the window of the coach, and there stood an enormous panther, directly in our path, and in a half-crouching posture. The negro swung his hat, and yelled as if he were frightened out of his senses; and there was good cause for his fear, for the animal was not more than twenty feet from us. The monster gave one or two leaps into the grass, and there stood and eyed us very closely as we passed. If the driver was frightened, those within the carriage were no less so. We were none of us sorry to part company with the creature. We soon reached the tavern, and, as the landlord was beginning to take the harness from the horses, I told him the adventure. He instantly dropped the harness; and calling all the men, boys, and dogs that were near, they all started at their utmost speed. They soon found the beast, and followed him nearly all night; but he would not 'tree.'

We had a little adventure at this tavern, which might have shocked some of the refined boarders at the Astor House. I had observed a white counterpane spread upon the grass, covered over with fruit for the purpose of drying. On sitting down at the tea-table, the same article appeared as a table cloth; and, on going to bed, we found it put to its legitimate use.

29

We arrived at last at the town of Franklin, which was the county seat. Where the bed of the Missouri River now lies, the court-house then stood. Such have been the ravages of this unreliable stream that not a house in the then flourishing town is now standing. It was here that I obtained a perfect knowledge of the English language: at least, I was assured by an itinerant professor that he could make me a thorough grammarian in twelve lessons. As I took the required number, if I am not all that he promised me, it must be his fault, and not mine.

While in St. Louis, I bought a lot of land, for which I painted five hundred dollars' worth in pictures at their then current value. On leaving St. Louis, I left the lot in charge of an agent, with funds for the accruing taxes. I never thought of the lot or the agent for five years, when I met a gentleman in Washington who was well acquainted with real estate in St. Louis. I asked him if he knew anything about my lot: he said it had, he thought, been sold for taxes. This proved to be true; but, as the limit of redemption had not expired, I empowered this gentleman to redeem it, and to sell it at once, if he could get a fair price for it, to relieve myself from the trouble of looking after it. He sold it for seven hundred dollars. That same lot is now worth forty thousand. By such chances fortunes are made or missed!

My ambition in my profession now began to take a

higher flight, and I determined to go to Europe. I had accumulated over a thousand dollars in cash, and had bought a carriage and pair of horses. With these I started with my family for western New York, where my parents were still living, by whom we were warmly welcomed.

My success in painting, and especially the amount of money I had saved, was the wonder of the whole neighborhood. My grandfather Smith, at an advanced age, had followed his children to the West, and was living in the same place with my father. He had, as yet, said nothing congratulatory upon my success; but one day he began, 'Chester, I want to speak to you about your present mode of life. I think it is very little better than swindling to charge forty dollars for one of those effigies. Now I want you to give up this course of living, and settle down on a farm, and become a respectable man.' As I did not exactly coincide in his views, I did not become the 'respectable man' according to his notions.

My failure in Caledonia for four or five hundred dollars had caused as much surprise and excitement as would the failure of any of our first merchants in Boston. The surprise was, at least, as great to my creditors to find themselves paid off in full.

My plan now was to leave my wife and children with my father and mother, and go to Europe. This plan was so far matured and carried out that I had my trunk packed, and was to leave on the following morning.[1] Just before starting, my mother asked me to sit down by her, as she wished to have a serious talk with me. She began, 'You are now going to Europe; and how soon — if ever — you return no one can tell. You are leaving your wife and children with very little to live upon; certainly, not enough to support them in the way they have lived. To come to the point, I want you to give up your trip for the present, and buy a farm [pointing to one in the neighborhood that was for sale], and place your family in a comfortable position. If you go to Europe, and never return, they are then provided for; and this reflection will console you under any trials you may be called on to pass through.' This appeal was too much for me. I yielded; and the next morning, instead of starting for Europe, I started for the farm, and before night had a deed of one hundred and fifty acres. I next made a contract with a carpenter to build a frame-house upon it; and then started for Washington to spend the winter [1821–22].

I had fairly begun work before Congress assembled, and had some happy specimens for exhibition. I spent about six months there; was full of business, and was able in the spring to pay for the new house, and make another payment on the farm.

---

[1] The ship I was intending to sail in was the ill-fated Albion. She was wrecked, and all on board were lost except one man, an invalid, who was thrown up a cleft in the rocks and saved.

James Madison

CHESTER HARDING

The following summer I spent in Pittsfield and Northampton. Mr. Mills, United States Senator from Massachusetts, resided in the latter town. He had seen my pictures in Washington, and had spoken favorably of them and of me; and I found that I had already a high reputation. I at once got orders, and in a short time my room was tolerably well filled with pictures.

While I was there, the annual cattle-show came off. I allowed my pictures to be exhibited among the mechanic arts. They elicited great admiration, and formed one of the chief attractions. I went into the room one day when there was a great crowd, and was soon pointed out as the artist. Conversation ceased, and all eyes were turned upon me. This was altogether too much for my modesty, and I withdrew as quickly as possible.

I one day received an invitation to a large party, to be given by Mrs. Ashmun (the stepmother of George Ashmun), which I accepted; but, as the evening drew near, began to regret that I had done so. I finally went into my room, and sat down on the bed, before beginning to dress, and took the matter into serious consideration. Should I go? or should I not? It was a fearful ordeal to go through. I had never been to a fashionable lady's party, and should not know how to behave. My heart grew faint at the thought of my ignorance and awkwardness. But then, I reflected, there must be a first time; and, with a mighty effort, resolved

33

that this should be it! So I went, and passed through the trial better than I anticipated; but I was glad enough when it was over.

While in Northampton, I painted the portraits of two gentlemen from Boston. They encouraged me to establish myself in that city [1823]. I did so, and for six months rode triumphantly on the top wave of fortune. I took a large room, arranged my pictures, and fixed upon one o'clock as my hour for exhibition. As soon as the clock struck, my bell would begin to ring; and people would flock in, sometimes to the number of fifty. New orders were constantly given me for pictures. I was compelled to resort to a book for registering the names of the numerous applicants. As a vacancy occurred, I had only to notify the next on the list, and it was filled. I do not think any artist in this country ever enjoyed more popularity than I did; but popularity is often easily won, and as easily lost. Mr. Stuart, the greatest portrait painter this country ever produced, was at that time in his manhood's strength as a painter; yet he was idle half the winter. He would ask of his friends, 'How rages the Harding fever?'

Although I had painted about eighty portraits, I had a still greater number of applicants awaiting their turn; but I was determined to go to Europe, as I had money enough to pay for my farm, and some sixteen hundred dollars besides. I had engaged to paint a few portraits in Springfield, which I did on my way to Barre, New

34

York, where my family were living. After spending a week or two there in arranging matters connected with their comfort, I took leave of them, and started for New York city, where I was to embark. On my way, I spent a day or two in Northampton with my friends. While there, a lady,[1] whose judgment I respected, advised me to send for my family, and establish them in that town; urging as a reason, that my children would grow up wild where they were, and that my wife could not improve in the accomplishments of refined society, but would inevitably remain stationary, on the standard level of those she would be obliged to associate with, while I should be improving, by mingling with the refined and distinguished persons my profession would throw me among. I was impressed with the good sense of this advice, and adopted it. I started at once for my wild home, and brought my family, now numbering four children, to Northampton, and saw them well settled in a very excellent boarding-house, where they remained two years. I have had good reason to thank my friend for her judicious suggestion.

And now, at last, I took my departure for a foreign land, leaving wife, children, and friends — all, indeed, that I had sympathy with — to cast in my lot, for a time, with strangers in a strange land. My heart was full of conflicting emotions. Scores of my patrons in Boston had tried to dissuade me from taking this step,

[1] Mrs. Joseph Lyman.

some urging as a reason, that I already had such a press of business that I could lay up a considerable sum of money yearly; while others insisted that I need not go abroad, for I already painted better pictures than any artist in this country, and probably better than any in Europe. My self-esteem was not large enough, however, to listen to all this, and my desire for study and improvement was too great to be overpowered by flattery. In spite of all advice to the contrary, I sailed for England, in the good packet ship Canada, on the first day of August, 1823.

During the two years of separation from my family which ensued, I kept a journal to send to my wife; and, as it gives the details of my experiences on the other side of the Atlantic with greater freshness than I could throw into any account I might try to give at this distance of time, I shall continue my narrative by making extracts from it.

CHAPTER III

THAT Mr. Harding's career had excited a widespread
and unusual interest, is evidenced by many tributes to
his genius written at that time, which still exist. As
early as June 29, 1823, before he went to England,
Samuel Orne, Esq., of Springfield, Massachusetts, wrote
regarding him to his brother-in-law, Hon. D. A. White
of Salem, Massachusetts, as follows:

Mr. Harding's three weeks were up yesterday, in which
time he has painted fifteen portraits, one of which is an excellent one of himself. He has also painted Judge Hooker, Mr.
G. Bliss, Mr. Sprague, Mr. Ames, and Mr. Pyncheon, besides
those he had begun when you were with us. I sent you the
last 'Journal,' containing a most ridiculous puffing article, for
you to laugh at, written by the editor, from which I should
think Harding would have received anything rather than
pleasure. As to the likenesses, however, they are admirable,
and the painting I should consider first-rate. The difficulty
seems to be to decide which is best; the majority, however,
vote the Parson's [Rev. W. B. O. Peabody] to be, and mine the
least striking at first, but *improves the most on acquaintance.*
Hang it, why can't it be so with the original! . . . Mr. Harding, I feel more and more interest in the more I see him. In
addition to his wonderful genius, and his natural good sense,
he has that frank, generous, open-hearted, unaffected manner, which at once secures a strong hold on your best feelings.

J. Stoddard Johnston, Esq., of Frankfort, Kentucky,
writes in 1881 to Samuel Bowles, Esq., of Springfield,
Massachusetts:

CHESTER HARDING

The receipt of your letter reminded me that I had seen contemporary mention of Mr. Harding in some old family letters. I have succeeded in finding the one in which he is mentioned, and transcribe it, as of probable interest. It is written by my great-grandfather, in New York, to his daughter, my grandmother, in New Orleans.

'March 25, 1824

Calling at Mr. Dwight's office yesterday, he mentioned a curious fact of an American artist, a portrait painter of eminence, Chester Harding, about five years ago destitute of home and hope. . . . Last August he sailed for Liverpool, and is now in London. He has painted Mr. Rush and lady, Mr. Perkins, Mr. Coke, the great, wealthy agriculturist, and his family, the Duke of Sussex, and is patronized by the Duke of Gloucester. He has written for permission to exhibit the portrait of our minister, Mr. Rush, in our Academy. It is probable that he will meet with the greatest success and reward in England, that great mart of encouragement for the arts and sciences. This is so astonishing an instance of original genius rising superior to want of education and absolute penury, that I have thought it a better topic for your gratification than occupying the same number of lines with mere inanity.'

The allusion to himself, referred to by Mr. Harding in a letter to his wife, somewhat later, is also introduced here. It is taken from 'Blackwood's Magazine' for August, 1824, under the head of 'Portrait Painting':

CHESTER HARDING

This extraordinary man is a fair specimen of the American character. About six years ago, he was living in the wilds of Kentucky, had never seen a decent picture in his life, and spent most of his leisure time, such as could be spared from the more laborious occupations of life, in drumming for a militia company, and in fitting axe-helves to axes, in which

Charles Sprague, Cashier of the Globe Bank,
Boston

two things he soon became distinguished. By and by some revolution took place in his affairs; a new ambition sprang up within him; and being in a strange place (without friends, and without money, and *with* a family of his own), at a tavern, the landlord of which had been disappointed by a sign painter, Mr. Harding undertook the sign, apparently out of compassion to the landlord, but in reality, to pay his bill, and provide bread for his children. He succeeded; had plenty of employment in the 'profession' of sign painting, took heart, and ventured a step higher — first in painting chairs, and then portraits. Laughable as this may seem, it is nevertheless entirely and strictly true....

Mr. Harding is now in London; has painted some remarkably good *portraits* (not pictures); among others, one of John D. Hunter (the hero of 'Hunter's Narrative'), which is decidedly the best of a multitude; one or two of H.R.H. the Duke of Sussex, the head of which is capital; one of Mr. Owen, of Lanark — a portrait of extraordinary plainness, power, and sobriety; and some others which were shown at Somerset House and Suffolk Street.

Mr. Harding is ignorant of drawing. It is completely evident that he draws only with a full brush, correcting the parts by comparison one with another. Hence it is that his heads and bodies appear to be the work of two different persons, a master and a bungler. His hands are very bad; his composition, generally, quite after the fashion of a beginner; and his drapery very like block-tin, or rather, I should say, this *was* the case, for there is a very visible improvement in his late works.

A. B.

Upon Mr. Harding's departure for England, Miss Louisa J. Park, of Boston, afterwards the wife of E. B. Hall, D.D., addressed to him the following lines:

> Is there no magic in the works of men?
> Sits there no spirit, Bryant, on thy pen?

CHESTER HARDING

Doth Allston commune but with earthly things?
Is it no witchcraft that round Harding flings
The mighty power to chain Expression down,
And sketch with equal truth the sage or clown?
How from his rapid touch the features grow,
And on the senseless canvas living glow!
While gentler strokes shade each defect away,
Yet let the fixed and close resemblance stay!
Most wondrous gift, from nature's self derived,
His genius of all foreign aid deprived,
Sprung up and bloomed amid our wilds obscure,
And won its self-taught way to glory sure.
No Grecian temples caught his boyish eye,
In youth, he gazed on no Italian sky,
But taste untutored claimed her favorite child,
And heaven-born Genius led him from the wild.
Soon shall the deep blue waves beneath him heave,
And brighter lands his pilgrim steps receive.
Soon shall the noblest trophies of his art
Wake the deep raptures of his feeling heart;
But, oh! still homeward may his wishes turn;
To gild his country's fame, each talent burn!
Crowned with success, uninjured by his fame,
As erst our great, our modest Allston came,
Soon may he tread his native shores once more,
And find his perils with his wanderings o'er.

EXTRACTS FROM JOURNAL

1823, *August* 1. Left New York for Liverpool in the
ship Canada. Got on board the steamboat at the Bat-
tery wharf at 10 o'clock A.M., and on board ship at 12,
the ship having dropped down the harbor the night preceding. While my fellow-passengers were taking leave

of friends and relatives, I, being deprived of that compound of pain and pleasure, stood gazing, sometimes on the crowd that came to see us off, sometimes on the distant and delightful scenery that surrounds the harbor, and sometimes lost on silent meditations.

Ship weighed anchor at 4 P.M., and beat out against head winds.

August 6. Surrounded by waves mountain-high. Sometimes our ship plunged into the valley and then rose to the brow of an immense hill. We continued, however, to sail on in the centre of this apparent circle, which seemed to move on with us.

August 13. Saw a brig at a great distance. At 4 P.M. killed a porpoise, and took him on board. He appears more like flesh than fish; has a great quantity of blood in his frame, and about the jaws and neck resembles a hog.

August 14. High wind and rain, with a tremendous sea.

August 15. Gale so severe that I could obtain no sleep at night.

August 16. I was very much alarmed by the continued and increased violence of the gale, but I fancy without any real danger. While others slumbered in fearless security, I was busily occupied upon deck in seeing that all was rightly managed.

August 17. Greatly refreshed by a night of undisturbed sleep. Off Cape Clear, with a light breeze from the south. Sea very calm, with little rolling or pitching of the vessel, a pleasure, the enjoyment of which repaid us well for the suffering undergone for three days and nights, previously, during the beating inflicted by the gale. Strong hopes entertained among the passengers of being in Liverpool, Tuesday morning, the 19th, and many bets made on the subject.

August 18. Went on deck at 4 o'clock A.M., and found the sailors taking in sail. At half past four, saw the sun rise, and before half of its orb was visible it began to be hid by a black cloud. The whole sky looked awfully threatening. The captain seemed much agitated, and upon speaking with him, I found that we were in the Irish Channel, and within a short distance of the rock on which the unfortunate Albion was lost. This intelligence, with the recollection of how near I came to taking passage on board that vessel, occasioned not a little emotion. The captain kept pacing the deck amid a violent rain-storm, which had now commenced, and beat full in his face. This voluntary exposure did not lessen my fears. Soon, however, the clouds began to break and clear away. 12 o'clock, all well. At 4 P.M., take in a pilot.

August 19. As the sun rose, we discovered land; at 10 A.M., arrived safely in port [Liverpool], and felt so ridiculously happy in putting my foot on shore again that I laughed heartily, without knowing why.

The docks of this city are amazing to a stranger. The city has very narrow, dirty streets, over shoes in mud.

42

Went in search of the picture gallery, and after much trouble in searching found it, but there were few good pictures in it.

Stopped at the Waterloo Hotel, where everything is in fine style.

Wednesday, August 20. Took a seat at Liverpool in an opposition coach for Birmingham. Traveled through a delightful and highly cultivated country. Admired the neat and clean appearance of the cottages. The sudden and very great transition from ease and opulence to extreme and abject misery cannot fail, however, to be a source of painful reflection to every intelligent traveler upon that road. The rich seem to have almost exhaustless wealth from the refinement and profusion of their luxuries; and the squalid wretchedness of the poor exhibits not less striking evidence of the extreme of poverty. The first annoyance experienced by a stranger traveling in this country is the unremitting applications of coachmen, waiters, and chambermaids for money, when he is unable to discover any foundation for their claims. Custom, however, is so despotic a tyrant, and so irresistible in his sway, that one yields to all these demands without questioning their justice; the authority from which they are derived is so universally respected that its name is a sufficient passport for every species of imposition.

Birmingham, from its great number of mills, is enveloped in smoke; which, in addition to a fog, almost

43

prevents one from finding his way through the streets.

One of our fellow-passengers gave us (Captain Barnaby and myself) a letter to his friend in Birmingham, which contained a singular mistake, that amused us not a little. The letter ran, 'Dear Tom, will you show these gentlemen some of your manu*factures?*' instead of factories. The consequences of the mistake were such as might be anticipated. The note was duly delivered with our address, and in a very short time the 'man of brass' came down, quite out of breath, with many apologies for being out when we did him the favor to call, begging that we would accompany him to his warehouse, where he would show us as great a variety, and at as low prices, as any man in his line in Birmingham. But, alas! when informed by us of his mistake, and he ascertained that he should have no heavy orders to fill, he was instantly seized with an ague that seemed to freeze him into utter speechlessness: but a few moments sufficed to restore to him the use of his faculties, and his manners softened towards us sufficiently to induce an offer of his services in showing us some of the wonders of the town; an offer which was readily accepted, and which procured us the sight of one brass and copper foundry.

Friday, August 22. Left Birmingham for London.

Saturday, August 23. Entered the grand metropolis, and took lodgings at Cooper's Hotel. Walked about the neighboring streets; saw the mighty St. Paul's, and the millions passing it. On first entering Fleet Street, I

44

was disposed to stop until the crowd had passed, but soon found the procession was interminable. In the evening went to see Matthews in 'Mons. Tonson'; not so much gratified as when I saw him in Boston.

Sunday, August 24. Rain and smoke render a candle almost necessary to read or write. My friend left me to my own reflections, which my situation — being in a small, dark room in the third story, or, as my friend described it, 'the first floor down the chimney' — united to a gloomy day, conspired to make quite depressing. My only prospect from the windows was a sight of a few dirty buildings with their outhouses. Then the awful tolling of St. Paul's went to my heart with overwhelming power. I had never before heard such melancholy peals, and their first influence was irresistible. The clouds broke in the evening, and I walked down to the Waterloo Bridge.

Tuesday, August 26. Took a coach, and drove up and down the city in search of Mr. Leslie, without knowing his address; and, after two or three hours of fruitless exertion, and half a guinea coach hire, I accidentally cast my eye on the letter I had to him, when I saw, 'No. 8, Buckingham Street, Fitzroy Square.' I had the satisfaction of at length presenting my letter to him; but, finding him engaged, I soon left him, with the promise to call again in the evening. At tea, met Newton and Bowman and Mason, with whom I had a delightful conversation.

Wednesday, August 27. Accompanied Leslie to the Royal Academy, where I found many students at their 'devotions,' and saw one of Raphael's Cartoons, with copies of all of them. I was greatly disappointed in these renowned works, more particularly in regard to their coloring.

Thursday, August 28. Mr. Leslie having procured me a ticket of admission to the gallery of Mr. Angerstein,[1] I visited it, and saw there for the first time an original Vandyke: it was masterly indeed, and quite equaled my expectations. Saw many Titians, which failed in producing the same gratification; saw also several Claudes, all beautiful as Nature herself. There is here, likewise, a picture of the raising of Lazarus, by one of the old masters, which has been and still is extravagantly extolled, and which cost an enormous sum. Yet, notwithstanding its high reputation, and my endeavors to admire it because Leslie pointed it out to me, I could not think it very fine. I shall probably change my opinion of it upon a more extensive knowledge of the art, but I would give more for Mr. Allston's unfinished picture than for a score of such. Saw a fine Sir Joshua, and one of Wilkie — a Scotch merrymaking; delighted with both, as also Hogarth's 'Marriage à la Mode.'

[1] John Julius Angerstein, a Russian merchant established in London — born at St. Petersburg in 1735, died in 1822 — distinguished himself by his liberal patronage of the fine arts. After his death, his collection of paintings was purchased by the English government for £60,000, as the nucleus of a national gallery. — *American Encyclopædia.*

Washington Allston

CHESTER HARDING

September 1. Being my birthday, I had Mason to dine with me. After dinner, we went to see the grand gallery of the late Mr. West. From what I had already seen of his works, I was prepared to find his pictures quite inferior to what I once fancied them, and to the estimation of the public. Owing to this prepossession I was the more agreeably disappointed. 'Death on the Pale Horse' is awfully sublime, and I shrank back with horror when my eyes first glanced upon it. There were many others that delighted me, many which I thought quite ordinary, and some contemptible. I think that he has departed widely from nature in coloring, and that he has carried his classical ideas of the face almost to a deformity. If his heroes were to walk out of the canvas, and mingle in society, they would be found to resemble men of our day so little that they would scarcely be recognized as human beings. He was a great mannerist. His last pictures afford evidence of the decline of his intellectual powers.

Tuesday, September 2. Commenced the head of Mr. Baldwin for myself, and found that my hand was a good deal out. Leslie, Newton, and others being so curious to see my first picture, added not a little to the mingled feelings of doubt and confidence, hope and fear, which agitated and oppressed me.

Monday, September 8. Finished the portrait of Mr. Baldwin. Not entirely satisfied with it, but by no means discouraged; for I daily behold worse paintings than

47

I ever painted, even in Pittsburgh. Went to Vauxhall Gardens. I had never seen anything before resembling these gardens, and had no idea of the amusements they afford. Barnaby and I went about ten o'clock; and, in entering, took a long alley that was intentionally left very dark, and which opened directly into the quietest part of the garden. My astonishment upon leaving this dark alley was indeed beyond conception. There were, I suppose, ten thousand lamps, of various colors, most tastefully arranged, whose dazzling light bewildered, and, for a few moments, nearly blinded me, as they burst upon me, in contrast to the darkness I had left. In the centre of the principal part of the garden is an orchestra prettily fitted up with lamps and with fifty or more performers; there are also beautiful rotundas and long promenades. At every other place of amusement, such as the theatre, balls, etc., you see some thoughtful faces; but here every countenance is lit up with smiles, which give unequivocal evidence of participation in the enjoyment and magic influences of the scene. Splendid fire and water works were playing all the time. It was to me a scene of such perfect enchantment that I took no note of time; and it was near three o'clock before we left the gardens.

September 9. At night, taken violently ill of the cholera; thought of having occasion for an 'undertaker'; wished myself at home a thousand times in the course of a long and tedious night. The thought was dreadful to

48

me of the possibility that I might not see home again: the idea of dying away from home was horrible. This weakness did not leave me until I was out of danger. Morning at length came, and I got once more upon my feet; and, before night, obtained relief.

Thursday, September 11. Quite recovered my strength. Began the portrait of Captain Barnaby, and walked about the city.

Friday, September 12. Went to see the London Docks; saw a *wilderness* of masts; ships from every quarter of the globe; many from my own country, which I looked upon with uncommon pride and pleasure. I thought them infinitely the finest ships in dock. It was a charming sight.

Saturday, September 13. Went with Bowman to see Sir Thomas Lawrence's portraits. As much pleased as on the first visit. His women are angels, but his men are not so faultless by any means. There happened to be two or three learned critics making their remarks while we were there. It occurred to me, while listening to these gentlemen, that, however excellent a painter may be, it must take a long time to become known to the world; but, having once become celebrated, whatever he does is out of the reach of criticism: visitors go to see his works with a predisposition to be pleased with them. Very different is the case with the beginner. Instead of overlooking the faults, they are most apt to overlook any little merit the picture may possess, and seem to take

49

great credit to themselves for having discovered that the pictures are not perfect; but, happily for the artists, and perhaps for the art, the beginner is content with a smaller share of approbation, as he also is content with a small price for his first efforts. To criticise and praise judiciously requires great knowledge: to find fault is an easy task, as no work of genius is perfect. A young painter needs the criticism of the wise, that he may be confirmed in what is good in his work, and not merely to be made to feel that his work is bad.

Monday, September 15. Went with Mr. and Miss Leslie, and a party of ladies and gentlemen, to see the Dulwich Gallery. This is a splendid collection. The portrait of the Archduke Albert, by Vandyke, is the finest piece of art that I have yet seen; it is very nearly, if not quite, perfect; the shadows are so transparent that they do not appear at all at first glance. The portrait of Mrs. Siddons as the Tragic Muse, by Sir Joshua, is a fine picture; very yellow, perhaps too much so. Saw some of Claude's fine landscapes, and a multitude of other pictures, such as Cuyp, Poussin, Titian, Rembrandt, and some others, whose works are admirable: but then there are, as an offset to these beautiful pieces, hundreds of inferior productions, which to my mind are not worth the trouble of preserving, though they all in their turn find admirers. Some will admire a picture because it looks old; some, because it is so dark nothing is left to the eye, but all to the imagination; others, for the respect they have for the name of its author.

We then went to a beautiful spot of rising ground, about two miles from Dulwich, where we could see St. Paul's, and many other points of London. We had our fortunes told by some gypsies on our way. After walking about until four o'clock, we found ourselves seated upon the side of a hill, with our *déjeuner*, which was previously provided, before us: all ate as if it were his last meal. One of the greatest pleasures in this kind of feasting seems to be the delightful inconvenience which is unavoidable. In consequence of our choice of position, our plates and dishes would slip about in fine style: now a salt-cellar would begin its revolutions down the hill; now a glass of ale would follow its example, and perhaps a mustard-pot would turn a somersault or two; in short, we had every annoyance that can be necessary to render such an occasion charming. The ceremony of eating once over, and our legs straightened again, we adjourned to a level spot of grass that was like velvet, where we commenced a dance, which closed our amusements.

Sunday, September 21. My friend Barnaby kindly invited me to spend a week with him at his friend's, in Oxfordshire; so we mounted to the top of a coach, and, after traveling four or five hours in a hard rain, we arrived at our place of destination. The captain's friend, Mr. Large, is a gentleman farmer of some wealth, and much esteemed by all classes of society. Here I spent ten days, and I must say I never spent ten days more delightfully in my life. On the evening of our arrival, we were invited to a 'harvest-home': we met about fifteen gentlemen. When we first entered the room, I thought we were in a Yankee bar-room, so full was it of smoke. Every gentleman had his long pipe, that sent forth its blue encircling smoke most plentifully. The company, however, bore no likeness to the class that is found haunting our bar-rooms; they were mostly men of reading, and some of classical education. They were seated in a circle around a large fire, with a small table to each three or four; every man had his tumbler of hot toddy, of brandy, rum, or gin, as best pleased himself; and they were emptied often enough to keep the company in good heart. Songs and stories went round in rapid succession. At twelve o'clock we sat down to a plentiful supper; and at two went home, happy enough. . . .

Monday, September 29. Now came on the most delightful sport in the world. Mr. Large had invited about twenty ladies and gentlemen to take a day's sport, of coursing the hare. This, I found, was to show me a specimen of country sports. We went into the field in a martial manner, all well mounted; and we soon started a hare. The hounds were uncoupled, and after the little harmless creature they went like lightning, and the riders as close in the chase as possible. 'Here she is!' — 'There she goes!' — 'Now we have her!' — 'The hounds have lost the scent!' — 'No; they have it again!' and so on was the cry for ten or fifteen minutes, when the hounds came up with her, and soon dispatched her. In the course of the day we had seven or eight fine courses. One could hardly say which were most excited by them — the horses, the riders, or the dogs. At night, most of the gentlemen sat down to a dinner prepared for the occasion, which was a jollification indeed. We stuck to the table until three o'clock: we had toasts, songs, and a flood of the best wines the country could afford. The old parson was the man last at the table; and, while at it, would thump the hardest, drink the hardest, and laugh the loudest, of all the company. Thus ended my delightful visit.

EXTRACT FROM A LETTER TO JUDGE LYMAN OF NORTHAMPTON

'LONDON, *October* 10, 1823

'I have just returned from a Sunday visit in the country, where I mixed with farming gentlemen, country squires, and clergymen, and a pleasant visit it was. They are of the class I most wish to see. They are hospitable and frank in their manners, and mostly men of education, but of little general knowledge — rich, though few own the land they cultivate. It is owned by the lords and gentry, with few exceptions. The gentleman with whom we stayed is a great sheep-grower and farmer, keeps his horses and hounds for the accommodation of his friends, and drinks his old port every day, after dinner; in short, lives the kind of life that would not offend you or me in America. But, my dear sir, the parishes here are made up of everything undesirable that the imagination can paint. I will not go into detail, lest I tarnish the fair picture I have just drawn. . . . I laughed heartily when you spoke of my qualifications as a traveler, and compared me to the immortal Franklin. Would to God I were worthy to be named in the same breath with that great man!'

[When Mr. Harding sailed for England, he left his wife and four children in pleasant surroundings at Northampton, Massachusetts, under the patronage of his friend, Judge Lyman who, by the way, was the grandfather of Hon. Frederic A. Delano, one of the original members of the Federal Reserve Board. The friendship which existed between Judge Lyman and Mr. Harding has been continued by the association of some of their children and grandchildren.]

Monday, October 13. Went with Mason to Westminster Abbey; struck with amazement at this wonderful pile; the architecture is sublime, but, together with all that we associate with Westminster Abbey, it is impressive beyond the power of description.

Friday, October 17. Went to Drury Lane Theatre. In going into the pit in a tremendous crowd, had my pockets picked of five pounds: whoever took it must have been a finished master in the 'art and mystery

54

Judge Joseph Lyman, of Northampton,
Massachusetts

Grandfather of Mr. Frederic A. Delano, of Washington, D.C.,
and great-grandfather of Governor Franklin D. Roosevelt, of New
York

of pocket-picking.' My purse was in my pantaloons' pocket, and it was with great difficulty that I could get my own hand into it; but I suppose it was fished out with hooks that are prepared purposely. Saw Macready in 'Hamlet'; very great acting.

Sunday, October 19. At twelve, noon, reading by candle-light. A good deal afraid of taking the small-pox. I exchanged beds with the child that lies ill of it the day before the pox made its appearance on her.

Monday, October 20. Had a great disappointment in seeing the celebrated 'Chapeau de Paille,' by Rubens. I thought it had little, besides the name of its author, to recommend it to the lover of art. I think it vastly over-rated: had I seen it in a pawn-broker's window, with the price of five pounds affixed to it, I am certain I should have passed it without buying. The face is out of drawing, and the coloring by no means to my taste. I am almost sorry that I saw it. By the side of it, I saw the half-length portrait of an old woman (by Rembrandt) that was *living.* I would rather possess it than a score of the 'Chapeau de Paille.'

Thursday, October 30. Went to see the pictures by Sir [Joshua Reynolds], and the copies by the young students of London. Sir Joshua's pictures are splendid: they stand first, in my estimation, of all modern art. Much is said by the artists of the day, however, of their bad drawing and fading colors; so I must take another look or two before I make a decision. The more I learn of the system of copying even the greatest painters, the more I disapprove of it. Of this I am tolerably certain: that it is very absurd to put the inexperienced to copy these masterly productions. How these effects have been produced puzzles the oldest and best painters now living, and to put young scholars to copy these works is, in my opinion, like putting a boy to solve a knotty problem in algebra, before he knows his letters or figures. Had I a friend beginning to paint, he should not copy a picture unless it were to ascertain the colors that had been used, of which he might be in doubt.

EXTRACT FROM A LETTER TO C. M. H. (HIS WIFE)

'LONDON, *November* 4, 1823

'You cannot imagine how much I want the society of yourself and the bairns in this unsocial world; much of my time is spent in solitude. It is not the most desirable way of living I do assure you, yet it is as others live. You perhaps would like to know what my occupations and amusements are, and I can tell you in a few words. My time is chiefly spent between the study of French, history, and painting. My amusements are the theatres and sometimes, though seldom, I kill an hour with my friends. My principal pleasure is in anticipation. You have often heard me say that our pleasures live only in memory and hope, and I do assure you my greatest enjoyment is in the hope of again meeting my family and friends, and of deserving and receiving that patronage

56

my countrymen were disposed to extend to me before I left America. But this I am well aware of, that more will be expected and required of me than was looked for in me before leaving my country; in the same way as what would be considered an astonishing effort in a boy of fifteen would be but feeble in a man of thirty.

'You will not, I hope, think from my manner of writing that I am discouraged, for, be assured, it is not the case. I am pretty well convinced that I have nothing to unlearn: yet there are many things I have to guard against, the most prominent of which is an artificial taste, or a kind of antiquarian madness which seems to be very contagious, judging from the number of its victims. I have met them at different exhibitions, where I have heard them praise, in the most extravagant manner, and without discrimination, the worst as well as the finest of the works of the old masters. I have seen some of these that truly delighted me, and would as soon quarrel with a connoisseur for not admiring these excellent works, as I would for his admiration of the most indifferent of them. . . .'

Thursday, November 13. Began the portrait of Mr. Rush.

November 18. Finished it much to my own liking; it is my best head.

CHESTER HARDING

'LONDON, *November* 27, 1823

'. . . I never read your letters with such interest before; if you knew the pleasure they gave me, I am sure you would spin them out to a great length; you can mention nothing that will be uninteresting, coming from home and you.

'I am glad that you are so well pleased with the family and the society you live in, and beg you not to waste your time in mourning my absence, for it may be more wisely spent. . . . I am glad to know that you are about to commence the study of the French language, and I hope you will make greater proficiency in it than I do. My head is so full of painting that, while in England, I shall not excel in that elegant language, I fear, and, indeed, it is little matter if I know no other than my favorite language, which speaks to the understanding through the sense of sight.

'I have had an introduction to Sir Thomas Lawrence, through Mr. Rush, and find him a very polite, gentlemanly man. He expressed a wish to see one of my pictures, and promised to criticise it candidly; so a few days after, I carried him the head of Mr. Rush, which I have just finished, and my own, for his inspection. He looked at both for some time, without saying a word, during which time I was in awful suspense, but at length he spoke of them in very flattering terms. He asked in what school I had studied; I told him in the Stuart

58

school. I told him this that he need not think I wanted to pass for a prodigy. He then had a sitter, so after inviting me to call often and at all times, he left me to make such comparisons between his and my own pictures as I could. A few nights after, I met him at the Academy, where he was very polite. So much for this wonderful man. But I do not think, after all, that his heads of men are any better than some of Mr. Stuart's; Governor Strong's portrait, for instance.'

Monday, December 8. Spent Sunday evening at Mr. Rush's, where I met Mr. Owen, Mr. Hunter, and several other countrymen, as well as a number of Englishmen. Was highly pleased with Mr. Owen; and listened with deep interest for two hours to the conversation of Mr. Rush and Mr. Owen. It ran chiefly upon the new system of education adopted by the latter at New Lanark. The theory seems very feasible, and the successful experiments he has made at New Lanark leave little doubt of its usefulness. The system is thoroughly republican, and Mr. Owen says that the United States is the 'half-way house' between this country and his desired object.

Wednesday, December 24. Mr. Leslie continues to be as kind and friendly as ever; he never loses an opportunity of serving me in any way. If there are any collections of pictures, or lectures on art, he never fails of gaining me admittance, which to me is worth half the city besides. He smuggled me into Somerset House to-day to hear the annual lecture by Sir Thomas Lawrence. After a few words of congratulation to those who had just received the prizes for drawing and painting, the latter took a broad and general view of art, which he treated in a very interesting manner. He said much upon the comparative merits of modern masters. He eulogized Mr. West most highly. He is the best reader, Lewis Strong excepted, that I have ever heard, and is one of the best looking men in the world, with black or very dark brown eyes, and a fine, white polished forehead.

Thursday, December 25. Breakfasted with Hunter. Met Mr. Owen and other gentlemen. Mr. Owen invited me to dine with him at Mr. John Smith's, M.P. Here I felt painfully embarrassed, being conscious that I was in some measure the representative of my country, or that I might be taken as a specimen of Americans. The gentlemen present could know nothing of my history, and, of course, would set me down for just what I appeared to them: they did not even know that I was an artist. However, when I could say nothing to advantage, I listened attentively; and gained by the conversation, however much I failed to contribute to it.

Sunday, December 28. I am often vexed to hear the Americans abuse Mr. Hunter in the manner they do. I have spent much time in his company, and I think him one of the most remarkable men I ever knew. He left the Osage Indians about seven years ago, and brought with him none of the vices incident to a civilized people. He was raised among the Indians from infancy, and knew no other, nor wished for any better, way of obtaining a livelihood than that of chasing the buffalo and deer. Humanity prompted him to rescue a party of whites whom the Indians had doomed to destruction, by deserting his party, coming over to the whites, and putting them on their guard. In consequence of which he left his tribe and all the associations of his youth. He first went to school at the age of nineteen or twenty; and the proficiency that he has made in the various branches of scholastic education proves the absurdity of the common opinion, that a man at twenty is too old for studying the sciences, unless he has had the first principles beat into his head by schoolmasters. Mr. Hunter is a good English and, I am told, a good Latin scholar. He is qualified to practice physic; he is a good mathematician; in short, there is scarcely a branch of science that he has not made some proficiency in. His society is courted by the great, partly, no doubt, because he is a wonder; but the very thing that makes him wonderful is that which reflects his greatest honor. I think him an honor to the country that claims him, and I am happy to find that he is devotedly attached to that country. My own want of education I feel constantly, but with such an example before me, let me not complain. If knowledge is worth pursuing I think any man can obtain it.

January 7, 1824. Went last night to the theatre; saw

Madame Vestris in 'The Beggar's Opera.' She is one of the most angelic singers on the English stage; but she is one of the most abandoned of the female race, given up to every vice that can tarnish the female character: the bare mention of her name ought to bring a blush upon the cheek of modesty. To see such a woman cheered and applauded by a Christian audience is to me an unaccountable incongruity.

January 14. Began the portrait of His Royal Highness the Duke of Sussex. This was the first time that I ever had the honor of seeing one of the royal family; and, of course, my approach to this august personage was marked by some little palpitations of the heart: but his affable manners placed me entirely at my ease. In the course of the sitting, His Royal Highness spoke warmly of America, and said he felt a pleasure in being painted by an American artist. In this country, it is looked upon as a mark of great distinction to be allowed to paint one of the royal family. For this honor I am indebted to my friend Hunter. The duke is a prodigiously fat man, above six feet high, of very uncommon features, but not intellectual.

Monday, January 19. Finished the portrait of the duke. He seems well pleased with it, and seems to take considerable interest in my success. All who have seen the portrait think it the best that ever was taken of His Royal Highness.

His Highness gave me a ticket to the Highland So-

Harrison Gray Otis

ciety's dinner, an annual jubilee from time immemorial. This was the grandest affair I ever had the pleasure of witnessing. Some two hundred of the Highland chiefs and lairds, all in their appropriate costume, were assembled. Every man wore the plaid of his clan. There were five or six of us in black coats: we were placed at the foot of one of the long tables, and had a fine view of the company. Old and young were splendidly dressed, and a gorgeous sight it was. After the regular toasts, such as 'The King,' 'The Royal Family,' 'The Ministers,' and so on, volunteer toasts were given. The Duke of Sussex was the president, and was addressed as the Earl of Inverness; the clans considering that title higher than his English one.

At intervals, I tried to make some conversation with my black-coated neighbors; but their attention was apparently too much absorbed by what was going on at the other end of the table. Presently I saw the duke's servant coming down to our end of the table, and, approaching me, said, 'His Royal Highness will take wine with you.' I rose, and His Royal Highness half rose and bowed. Such a mark of distinction was felt by my taciturn neighbors. I found them sociable and very respectful after that. As soon as the dinner was dispatched, the bagpipes were introduced, and the first note started the company to their feet, and nearly the whole assembly joined in the 'Highland Fling.' Many songs were sung: Miss Payton, afterward Mrs. Wood, sang some Scotch

63

songs from the gallery. It was an exciting scene, and continued till a late hour. Some were 'fu',' and all were 'unco happy.' As the duke retired, he honored me with a shake of his hand.

CHAPTER IV

January 20, 1824. Set off for Holkham, Norfolk, to paint the portrait of Mr. Coke — a period of great anxiety.

January 21. Arrived at Holkham at ten in the evening. Rang at the door, and was answered by a footman in powder, who announced me to the next servant; and my name rang through the long hall most awfully. One of the head servants then asked me if I would go to my room, or be introduced to the family. I chose the former. Next morning I went down to breakfast with trembling steps. As I passed through the long range of splendidly furnished apartments, the echo of the shutting doors, and even my own steps in these large rooms, was frightful; and what rendered my embarrassment greater was that I had never seen Mr. Coke, and had to introduce myself. At length, however, I reached the breakfast room, and was ushered into it. There were but a few persons in the room, and neither Mr. Coke nor Lady Anne were present. They soon came in, and broke the painful silence I was constrained to observe. We soon were seated at table to the number of five and twenty ladies and gentlemen, the latter in their shooting dresses. Here I felt a little awkward, as the table arrangements were very different from any I had seen. In the centre of the room was placed a long table, around which the

65

company were seated; and side-tables, loaded with cold meats and cold game, were resorted to by any one who wished for flesh or fowl. It struck me at first as being a queer sort of hospitality not to be asked to take this or that, but left to help myself or go without. Each calls for coffee, tea, or chocolate, as he fancies, without being asked which he prefers. After breakfast, I joined the shooting party: we set off in terrible array, with guns, dogs, and game-keepers; the older gentlemen mounted on horseback. In the course of the day, I shot about a dozen in all — pheasants, partridges, and hares; and was withal excessively fatigued. They never shoot at game at rest. If a hare should stand in fair view within their shot, they would start him and shoot as he ran. In like manner they warn the birds of their danger. At six, we sat down to a sumptuous dinner. The very men with whom I had been shooting and conversing freely all day had so changed the 'outer man,' by throwing off their shooting habiliments, and putting on their finery, that I hardly recognized a single face at table. Every dish was of silver, gold knives and forks for dessert, and everything else about the table of corresponding costliness. The ladies retired about eight; and the gentlemen, with a few exceptions, gathered around a smaller table, and sat until nine, and then joined the ladies and took coffee. After coffee, some of the company retire to their rooms; others to side-tables to write letters; and such as have nothing else to do play whist or chess, or some

66

other games, until ten, when a supper is served up on a side-table, where the company stand, and eat or drink what they wish. After supper, one after another calls for a bedroom candle, and goes to his room. None stop later than eleven o'clock.

January 23. Began the portrait of Mr. Coke, after which I amused myself by sauntering about the gallery. I found many excellent paintings, a fine statue gallery, and a splendid library. Mr. Coke is said to have one of the finest manuscript libraries in the kingdom.

The furniture of this house is in the most extravagant style. Lady Anne showed me the state rooms, bed-rooms, etc., which are magnificent. The bed-curtains of one of the beds cost eight guineas a yard; the rest of the furniture was equally costly. All the principal rooms are hung with tapestry. I had no idea of the wealth of an English gentleman until I came here. Mr. Coke owns seventy thousand acres of productive land.

Mr. Coke is now, and always has been, an ardent admirer of America. He was the first to propose the recognition of our independence in the House of Commons. He is seventy-two years old, but retains all the mental vigor of a man of forty. He has, within two years, married a young wife of eighteen; and has by her a fine son to prop and support his declining years, and to inherit his large estates.

Wednesday, January 28. Commenced the portrait of Lady Anson — a daughter of Mr. Coke — upon a small

67

scale. We breakfast at ten, lunch at two; and at six the party assemble in the drawing-room, in full dress, for dinner. Mr. Coke leads the lady of highest rank first; then follows the highest titled gentleman with Lady Anne, and the rest fall in according to rank or seniority. I am a good deal bothered with the titles we have here. 'Your ladyship' and 'Your lordship' do not slip readily from my tongue.

There is great splendor in the dinner service, as well as in the attendants at table, of whom there are eight or ten in powdered livery as well as two out of livery — the one, the butler; the other, a sort of master of ceremonies.

There is a large bell in one of the towers of the hall, which is rung to announce the hours of breakfasting and dining. After breakfast, each lady goes to her room; and she enjoys entire freedom as to the disposition of her time during the day. Some order their carriages or horses, and drive or ride around the park. The gentlemen always go out shooting, unless they are prevented by bad weather.

Friday, 30. Finished the portrait of Mr. Coke. The family are highly pleased with it. Began the portrait of Lady Andover's daughter. Mr. Adair, one of our visitors, has been ambassador at Constantinople — a very pleasant gentleman.

Mr. Coke is most decidedly American in his feelings: he often says it is the only country where one spark of

68

freedom is kept alive; and he regrets very much not having gone over at the termination of the revolutionary struggle, that he might have seen the brightest character that ever adorned the page of history.

Friday night, some itinerant jugglers came to the Hall to amuse the family. Their performance was indifferent enough; but it was interesting to see the household collected. There were about seventy domestics. After the performance, Mr. Coke told the steward to give them a couple of guineas, and send them away.

February 1. Commenced the portrait of Mr. Blakie, Mr. Coke's steward, on the kit-cat size, at thirty guineas.

Lady Anson has a most benevolent heart; she spends much of her time, and a good deal of her money, amongst the poor and destitute of the neighboring village. Mr. Coke has very humanely provided for the servants who have grown gray in his service, by building them neat little cottages near the Hall, with a small piece of ground attached for a garden; and, in some instances, he has given a pension for life. They seem as happy as men can be in this life. They are seen every day about three o'clock walking up to the Hall for their dinners. They, with the steward and a few other of the upper servants, dine together as sumptuously as their master.

London, February 28. Went to the Italian Opera House to witness the performance of a grand oratorio. Madame Catalani was the principal attraction; the power of her voice far surpasses that of any singer I ever heard before. Besides sacred pieces, which she gave to admiration, she sung 'God save the King' and 'Rule Britannia'; and she so riveted my attention that I knew not what I did. I shouted 'Rule Britannia,' etc., as loud and as loyally as the best Englishman present. There were one hundred and forty performers, vocal and instrumental. The house is magnificent; there are four rows of boxes, all hung with red curtains, and splendidly upholstered.

On Thursday night I received a ticket from the Duke of Sussex to attend a dinner in support of old and indigent Jews, and for the education of the young; the duke in the chair. There were about two hundred present. After the cloth was removed, and the usual toasts drunk and speeches made, the school of children was introduced to the number of fifty. Each had some specimen of his skill in mechanics in his hand, a chair or shoes, etc. One of the little girls, about eight years old, and of most interesting appearance, recited a piece of poetry which had been written for the occasion. The lines were full of pathos, and delivered with astonishing force. This little manœuvre had a most powerful effect upon the company. The duke rose to speak; but his heart was so touched that he could not give utterance to his thoughts. Tears ran down his cheeks in a flood. He at length regained his self-possession, and spoke very feelingly, which had the effect desired — it drew tears from the

*Stephen Van Rensselaer, the Last of the
Patroons*

audience, but not such as the duke shed; these were from the purse instead of the eye. Twenty-three hundred guineas were collected.

The Duke of Sussex is a much better speaker than his brother York, whom I heard at the 'Theatrical Fund' dinner; but he is not an eloquent nor a strong-minded man. His goodness of heart, however, makes ample amends for all want of brilliancy.

Monday, March 15. Went to the House of Lords; and, through the kindness of the Duke of Sussex, was fortunate enough to get a front seat, on the foot of the throne — a place set apart for the sons of noblemen and foreign ambassadors. The debate, upon the recognition of the independence of South America, was extremely interesting. The Marquis of Lansdowne was the mover of the question, and he supported it most ably and eloquently; but, as it was a party question, his eloquence was in vain: the motion was lost by a large majority. The house is as uninteresting within as it is without. The custom of seating the lord chancellor on the woolsack is too ridiculous and barbarous for the present stage of civilization. There are three sacks, about ten feet in length, two feet high, and perhaps four feet wide, so put together as to form three sides of a square; the lord chancellor sits on the centre sack, the clerks on the others. The wigs which the lords wear are still less dignified in their appearance.

CHESTER HARDING

TO C. M. H.

'London, *March*, 1824

'. . . This is to me a most interesting period as you will readily imagine, when I tell you that to-morrow is the day for sending my portraits for exhibition. You know, already, the pictures I have painted for that purpose, namely, the duke, Coke, Perkins, Hunter, Rush, and Owen, some of which I intend to send to the new Exhibition in Pall Mall, which opens, for the first time this season, under the patronage of the Duke of Sussex. As many of my sitters have sat frequently to different artists, and have at different times been exhibited, I may fairly calculate upon a little jealousy and a great deal of severe criticism from the artists themselves, or their friendly or hireling critics. There is to be a likeness of the duke by Lonsdale, a full length in his Coronation Robes, in the new Exhibition, which will bring me in direct contact with him: at the same time it will give him the advantage, "as fine feathers make fine birds." Mr. Coke has been painted by Sir Thomas Lawrence, as well as by Lonsdale and a score of other painters. But why borrow trouble or be anxious? Why tease myself about what is out of my control? Ought I in reason to expect to have my pictures stand the comparison with these old practitioners? Whatever I may aim at ultimately, I should deceive myself did I for an instant suppose my pictures equal to those of the first artists in London.'

72

CHESTER HARDING

Saturday, April 10. Breakfasted with Mr. Owen. He is very confident of success in his attempts at universal reform. He is plain in his appearance, and simple in his manners, but strong in argument.

Monday, April 19. Went with Mr. Neale and Mr. Humphries to Greenwich Fair, about six miles from town. We got into a boat at Westminster Bridge and had a most charming sail down the Thames. Some thousands of town and country folks were assembled, and enjoying themselves in every variety of way. In addition to the Smithfield amusements, they have a singular mode of amusing themselves by rolling down a very steep and grassy hill: boys and girls are seen rolling and tumbling together in every direction and position.

The grand Hospital for Decayed Seamen is situated here. The building itself is extremely beautiful, and the effect is enhanced by the river which washes one side of the grand area; the surrounding landscape, harmonizing so well with the whole, renders the scene enchanting. It is delightful, too, to know that two thousand invalids are sharing a nation's gratitude. One sees contentment reigning in the faces of hundreds who are deprived of half their limbs. They are well-fed and well-clad, in a half-military uniform.

Monday, April 26. Commenced the portrait of Mr. Henry Anson. Delightful weather. Sunday called with Hunter upon the Duke of Sussex. He was very polite and kind. Mr. Hunter and I took a long walk, and

thought and talked about our country; compared it to
England: the result was favorable to the land of our
birth. In the course of our rambling, we got into a boat,
and floated with the tide from the Waterloo Bridge to the
Iron Bridge. On the Thames we had a most beautiful
view of the city. The sun was just setting, but still shone
bright upon St. Paul's stupendous dome, and some other
prominent points of the city, such as Somerset House,
the Adelphi, etc.; and, as we floated along under the
several bridges, which never look so strikingly grand
as when seen from beneath, we concluded it would be
many years before our country could boast such monuments of art. In viewing Waterloo Bridge, we were led
to speak of the event which this stupendous work per-
petuates; from that, to the captivity of Napoleon; of the
indelible stain that event has cast upon the great con-
queror of the age — what magnanimity he had it in his
power to show by treating this once powerful but now
fallen foe like a Christian, instead of dooming him to
waste his life in exile like a pirate.

Thursday, April 29. Dined with Mr. Everett; met
Mr. and Mrs. Appleton and others; a pleasant party.

Spring is now opening, and all nature seems to smile
again; fruit-trees in full blossom. How delightful to the
eye, after being shut up in fog and smoke for six months,
to see the green fields once more displaying their
charms! But spring approaches so gradually here that
one does not feel that pleasure which one feels in the

74

Northern States of America, where the transition from snow to verdure is so quick, that, before one can say spring approaches, it is already arrived. How delightful to meet old and intimate friends in a foreign land! Dr. Robbins and wife and Miss Pickard, who have just arrived, make me forget that I am in a strange country.

Saturday, May 1. Began the portrait of the Rev. ——, recommended by Leslie. He is a country clergyman; and, from his Jewing disposition, I should judge he had more taste in tithes than pictures. He spent at least one hour of his precious life in a fruitless attempt to lower my price.

I feel myself improving in every picture I paint. Nine tenths of the pictures that are painted in London are execrably bad.

Monday, May 3. Somerset House opened this day. This is a grand display altogether. Portraiture is the branch of art in which the English School stands preeminent. Sir Thomas Lawrence, Jackson, Shee, Phillips, Sir William Beechy, and one or two others, stand high; but Sir Thomas towers above them all. In the small cabinet pictures, after Wilkie, Leslie stands first. His picture of Sancho Panza in the apartment of the duchess is a beautifully told story, and commands great admiration. He devoted six months of hard study to it, and it was time well spent. Newton has a very clever picture of the 'Patient in spite of Himself,' which evinces more talent than industry in the author. He affects a con-

75

tempt for the minutiæ of his pictures, and, instead of giving them an agreeable finish, leaves them undetermined in the outline, and unfinished in effect. My own portraits do not look as well as I thought they would: they want the broad effect so necessary in this exhibition. On going into the room, I wished there was to be another exhibition immediately, that I might shun the defects in my next that I saw so plainly in these. The greatest advantage I shall derive from this exhibition is the opportunity of comparing myself with others. It was sickening, on first going into the room, to see some of my pictures so badly placed; but, on a little reflection, I thought I was placed as well as I deserve.

TO S. F. L.

'LONDON, *May* 10, 1824

'This is a lovely season, all the gayety of the kingdom is now in full bloom; the parks and gardens are green and inviting. It is one of the most delightful walks in the world to go into Hyde Park and Kensington Gardens at this time of year. It is the fashion here to go to the Park every day at five or six o'clock and make as great a show as possible. Those who keep their carriages never fail of displaying them, and those who do not, figure as pedestrians only. It is about a mile from one side of the Park to the other — I mean the part which is most frequented. There is a graveled way for the carriages and horses, by the side of which is a beautiful hard gravel walk for those on foot, divided from that for the carriages by a railing. There are from one to two thousand elegant carriages at the same time, in this fashionable procession, in fine weather, and from fifty to a hundred thousand people of all countries, ages, sexes, and colors, promenading the foot-walk, or sauntering across the green. But upon retiring from this show to my own room and to serious reflection, I am always struck with the folly of this gay rabble, and it never fails to create a longing for home and those happy scenes in domestic life, which the world of fashion are strangers to.

'I go every day to the different galleries and am both delighted and instructed. My own pictures in Somerset House are not in a favorable light, but that I expected. My friends, Leslie and others, say they are entitled to better places, which is some consolation.

'. . . I do not doubt if I were to remain here I could establish a permanent character as a painter, and here, of all places in the world, is the artist best paid for his labors. But, if I could in five years rise to be President of the British Academy with a "Sir" tacked upon my name, I would not forego the pleasure of living in America.'

May 13. Obtained a ticket of admission to the Marquis of Stafford's collection, which admits me every Wednesday of this and next month. A fine collection, containing many of the old masters.

77

Monday, May 17. In the evening, went to the opera;
saw a part of an Italian opera, and an English afterpiece.
In the course of the evening Madame Catalani sung
three songs, which were delightful, and of course were
encored. The entrance to the house is in the Haymarket;
and, an hour before the doors opened, the rush was so
great that I really thought my life in danger, women
screaming, men swearing and fighting. My friend
Barnaby and I took our seats in the pit; and, as we were
waiting for the performance to begin, we were standing
upon the benches, when an insolent fellow crowded between us, or rather crowded the captain out of his seat.
As the captain was a small man, I took the liberty of
hoisting the intruder out pretty roughly. Nothing but
my size saved me from a row.

Thursday, 20. Dined with Mr. Bowker. Met several
gentlemen of the bar; also Mr. Cox, a very amusing
poet; heard many pleasing anecdotes. Before dinner
went to see the grand display of gentry and nobility.
This was the grand drawing-room of the palace of St.
James. A line of carriages stretched from the foot of St.
James Street to the top of Bond Street, all in their
grandest trappings. I crowded my way, or rather was
forced down by the current, to the bottom of St. James,
where I stood for a half hour looking on like the rest of
the astonished multitude. The courtiers would in the
most condescending manner allow the crowd to see them
through the windows of their carriages, whilst their faces

Thomas Cooper, English Actor

seemed to express the greatest contempt for the plebeian rabble. I felt a good deal vexed, but relieved myself, as soon as the crowd allowed me to withdraw from a place where I should have been ashamed to have been seen by any of my acquaintances.

June 5. A call from Mr. Coke, the Duke of Norfolk, and General Fitzroy. This attention on the part of Mr. Coke is most gratifying.

TO C. M. H.

LONDON, *June* 7, 1824

'The long-looked-for letter has at last reached me; indeed, I had begun to be very impatient. You will hardly believe me when I tell you that when I opened your letter and saw the token of affection from little Caroline,[1] my heart grew very restless, and I have no doubt my face was colorless for a moment. I don't know how it is, but I never open a letter from home without a slight emotion of the heart; nor is that emotion quieted until I read the cheerful words, "We are all well." ...

'You are anxious, no doubt, to know how I am getting on in pecuniary matters. I can tell you that it costs me full twice the sum to live here that I had calculated on, but so long as I can keep the original stock (of money) whole I feel no uneasiness on that score. I have some portraits all the while on hand, and were I to attend more to the *shop* and less to the exhibitions, I doubt not

[1] The eldest daughter, afterwards Mrs. John L. King, of Springfield, Massachusetts.

79

but I could find as much business as I could do. But as money-making was not the object of my visit, so long as I can see my way clear, I shall not sacrifice the advantages this metropolis affords for the accumulation of a little trash that at present I do not stand in need of. I mean the little I could accumulate in the short time I shall stay in this country would be trash compared with the stock of mental riches that, with a moderate share of industry, I might treasure up. . . .

'Yesterday I, with a friend, got on a coach and went to Richmond, a place about seven miles from here, which has long been celebrated for its beauty of scenery. But, upon my soul, I could not find anything particular to admire but the cultivation and the appearances of comfort in the dwellings, as we walked about them. You are now living in a place a thousand times more beautiful (Northampton, Massachusetts), and as to grandeur of scenery there is no comparison. But art has made up the deficiencies of nature. Cultivation is brought to a very great degree of perfection here. It will be many years before we can vie with this country in that particular, and I must say it will be a long time before I shall wish to do so. This show is at the expense of nine tenths of the inhabitants, perhaps ninety-nine hundredths. Yet if contentment be riches, the lower order of peasantry are rich. I never saw any wrangling in all the various mobs which I have seen collected on different occasions. There seems to be in these lower orders a social and friendly disposition, which I am sorry to say does not exist in our country. There, on such days as an Election or General Review, the lower classes of society consider themselves licensed to get drunk, and render themselves as beastly as possible; and I hardly remember an instance of a holiday of the kind to pass over, without a fight and sometimes a dozen of them. I have not, while I have been in this country, seen anything in the streets, at the fairs, or any other place of amusement for the peasantry, that looked like ill-will toward each other. If I, in passing the crowd in the streets, happen to run against a boy, or tread upon his foot (which you know could not be a gentle pressure), he directly pulls off his hat and begs pardon, or at least makes no complaint. Not so at home. If one happens to encroach upon the rights of one of our republican boys in any degree, he lets fly a volley of mud rockets at you, and damns your eyes up and down.

'Tell Caroline that she is a good little girl for thus remembering her father, and that I thank her for the little lock she sent me. Assure the rest of the little ones that they are not forgotten by me.'

Monday, June 14. Went with Mr. Everett and family to Epsom Races. This was a grand affair; great crowd of vehicles of all sorts from a barouche down to a donkey-cart. We had our dinner with us, as is the custom with all, and a most sumptuous one it was — cold turkeys, chickens, champagne, etc.

81

CHESTER HARDING

Mr. Coke was at Somerset House, looking about without a catalogue, and pronounced the portrait of the Duke of Devonshire, by Sir Thomas Lawrence, and the portrait of Mr. Owen, by myself, to be the best in the room — so says Lady Anson. This pleased me much; at the same time I knew he was not correct; but such is the insatiable desire that man has for distinction, that he is willing to give ear to the most extravagant flattery, and will try hard to reconcile it to himself, however absurd it may be.

Sunday, June 20. Attended divine service at Westminster Abbey. The sermon may have been well or ill, it was all the same to me; my mind was completely absorbed in matters foreign to religious instruction. Yet I never in my life felt so sensibly the true sublimity of religion as I did while gazing on this wondrous pile. The organ fills one with devotional feelings; and it is impossible to look at the monuments and grandeur of architecture that surround one, without an elevation of feeling which bids earthly thoughts stand aside.

Sunday, June 27. Yet in doubt, whether it is my duty to stay another year in this country, or go home to my family and friends. Life is short at best: then why not spend it in a way that will be most conducive to our happiness while here? I have duties to perform towards my wife and four helpless children: ought I not, then, to live with them, and discharge those duties? These and the like thoughts are constantly haunting my mind. But then, I have made choice of a profession in which I am most anxious and determined to excel. The charm of distinction is dazzling my eyes continually. I have already excited a warm interest with many friends in my behalf: to fail, therefore, would be painful beyond description. To return to Boston and receive a cold welcome where I have been so warmly patronized would be a sore wound to my pride and ice to my ambition. Yet it is but fair to count upon this in some degree. Public favors and opinion are capricious. There was something novel, perhaps, in my history that contributed more to my unheard-of success than any merit I possessed as a painter. The fact of a man's coming from the backwoods of America, entirely uneducated, to paint even a tolerable portrait, was enough to excite some little interest. That source of interest will be cut off on my return. I shall be judged of as one having had all the advantages of the best schools of art in Europe; and the probability is, that more will be expected of me than is in the power of almost any man to perform.

TO S. F. L.

'LONDON, *July* 17, 1824

'... Have you heard much of Matthews? He has had a wonderful run. His Tour to America has brought crowded houses in all kinds of weather, but such a representation is, I am inclined to think, very prejudicial to us. The true character of our nation is but very little known here by, at least, nine tenths of the theatre-going people; consequently they are impressed with the notion that we are, as a nation, as truly represented by this buffoonery, as Monsieur Tonson, or any other of Matthews' favorite characters. He has introduced a Militia Review, at which there does not appear to be a great supply of arms, but pitch-forks, umbrellas, fishing-rods, etc., making up the deficiencies. Then the commanding officer reads the words of command, and so on, making the thing truly remarkable. This is well enough as a burlesque, but that the people should take this for the true picture of our Nation's Bulwark is, to me, quite ridiculous. A gentleman was asking me, the other day, many questions relating to America, and seemed well disposed toward us, but he said he thought we ought to have some military system, in order to defend ourselves against invasion. I replied that we had a military system. "What," he said laughingly, "your broomstick and umbrella men?" Yes, I told him, and that these broomstick and umbrella men had beaten the flower of the British army, twelve to one against them. (I here mentioned the affair at New Orleans.) This, I observed, was a home thrust to him, but it came in so opportunely, that, excited as I was at that moment, I believed it would have come out had I known that it would have cost me this gentleman's good-will, altogether.'

Saturday, July 31. Introduced to Irving, by Leslie.

84

He is very pleasing in his manners; talks with great volubility, at the same time has a little hesitation, or want of fluency, in conversation.

Called upon the Duke of Sussex. He recommends to me to send for my wife, and make England my home.

August 3. Called upon the Duke of Sussex, and got a letter to the Duke of Hamilton. On the 4th, gave up my rooms, and set off for Scotland. Arrived here (York) at half past nine, the 9th. It is with great difficulty I can understand the Yorkshire dialect. The cathedral here is sublime. I went to the top of the grand tower, which measures sixty-five feet square on the top, and affords one of the finest views of high cultivation that I ever saw. The cathedral is five hundred and twenty feet long. The town of York is a walled city: it has four public entrances through strong gates. Left York on Friday, at ten. The country is delightful. From London to York, and, indeed, in every other direction from London, the coachmen are fat and red-faced, answering faithfully the description given by Irving. They will certainly weigh from two hundred and fifty to three hundred pounds each; but, after leaving York for Scotland, the likeness is lost. They are like the coachmen of London, commonly called jarvies — dirty, and lean as greyhounds. The reason is, probably, that they have to take care of their own horses, as they drive only one stage.

Arrived in Glasgow at five on Sunday morning, August 8th.

Tuesday, August 10. Walked about Glasgow with my friend Pattison. Saw the Museum, the High-Church Cathedral, and many other objects of interest. This town is almost exclusively a manufacturing town — glass and cotton goods, but principally the latter.

Wednesday, August 11. Got into a coach with Pattison, and set off for New Lanark, the seat of Mr. Owen's great experiment. We arrived at Lanark about noon, where all was gayety. It was the annual fair. We dined with Mr. Owen at six o'clock. He lives in good style, keeps open house to those who visit his establishment, and everything is comfortable about him. The family is very interesting.

Thursday, August 12. Went down to the new village and through all the different mills. Heard the classes at their recitations; little boys and girls, from three to five, answering questions in geography. Mr. Owen asked a little creature, not more than four years old, what country I lived in, telling him the Atlantic divided my country from this. He first said the Brazils, then Columbia, then North America. The most perfect order prevails in every department of the establishment. The children are as happy at their lessons as they are at their play. Everything indicates contentment. The oldest class of boys is composed of those ten years old and under. They study natural history, botany, mineralogy, mathe-

Charles Carroll of Carrollton

matics, and music. Many of them perform well on different instruments: they dance four sets of cotillons at once; their dancing would not disgrace a London drawing-room. I never witnessed a more interesting sight than this.

To see children taken from the lowest dregs of society, and taught to enjoy all the blessings of refined life, and at an expense entirely within their own reach, is to every feeling mind a treat of the highest order. The parents of these children, and all above ten years old, work in the mills eight hours each day. Their pay enables them to buy every comfort that nature requires. There is a store here containing everything they want to eat, drink, or wear. The goods are laid in at the lowest rate, and cost and charges are all that is required for them. By this means, the goods are sold at thirty per cent lower rate than they would be otherwise. If, after the deduction of all the expenses of the establishment, there should be any money remaining, it is appropriated to the general good, such as buying medicines, paying physicians, etc.

The village is beautifully situated on the Clyde, with rugged and romantic scenery about it. The houses are built of stone; generally three, and sometimes four, stories high, with every convenience possible for cooking, etc.

Saturday, August 14. Went to the Falls of the Clyde, about two miles above New Lanark. The water falls about thirty feet perpendicularly, with beautiful scenery

87

around. About a mile from Lanark on the Courtland Craigs, a place famous for warlocks and witches in olden times, is the cave where Wallace hid himself.

There is at this time here a Mr. Flower from Indiana, who is authorized by Mr. Rapp of New Harmony to sell his establishment. Mr. Owen seems too credulous. Mr. Flower draws a 'long bow,' now and then; and has so far worked upon Mr. Owen as to persuade him to go out and see the place. Mr. Flower is all the time representing Indiana as the most important State in the Union. This I can see through readily enough, as he has a large estate adjoining New Harmony, which would be much improved by such a settlement as Mr. Owen would probably make. I advise Mr. Owen to try his plans in Massachusetts, or some other of the old States, where there is a more crowded population as well as a greater portion of intellect. But Mr. Flower will succeed, I fear.

Monday. Set off for Hamilton. Stayed at the inn. Tuesday morning, sent my letter with my address to the palace; but it was soon returned, with direction from the footman that 'all letters to his Grace must come through the post-office.' This, I afterwards learned, was to avoid refusing, more directly, admittance to the gallery, as there were so many applications that the family were constantly annoyed. I took the letter, and went to the palace with the resolve to see his Grace, if possible. After waiting half an hour, the duke came out from the breakfast-table, and very politely asked me into the breakfast-room, and invited me to take breakfast; but I declined the honor, and made my business known to him, which was to request the duke to sit for a picture for the Duke of Sussex. He readily complied, and asked me to send for my portmanteau, and take up my residence with him.

I soon commenced the portrait. The day passed off very happily in looking at the pictures of the old masters, of which there are hundreds. Five o'clock came, and I began to dress for dinner. Felt rather aguish from fear, and wished the ordeal of dinner well over. Six o'clock came at last, and I was ushered into the dining-room. In a short time I began to realize that my titled companions were very like other people; and in a short time more, my nerves became steady, though I could not entirely refrain from moving my knife and fork a little, or playing with my bread, or in some other awkward way betraying my want of ease. There was a display of great magnificence; servants all in livery, splendid plate. The duchess and her daughter retired early; and, about nine, the gentlemen followed them. The duchess made tea with her own fair hand, and was, besides, very agreeable. At half past eleven, I set off for bed; and, on my way, thanked my stars that it was all over, and matters stood no worse.

The palace is two hundred and sixty-five feet long by two hundred broad. The picture gallery is a hundred and thirty-five long, full of old cabinets and other curious furniture. I am obliged to own to myself that this style of living is very charming: everything around one savors strongly of title, wealth, and antiquity. We breakfast at ten, lunch at two, and dine at six. The duchess is pretty, witty, and sociable. Lord Archibald Hamilton is staying here at this time, and is a very clever man. I think I shall succeed very well. All the household servants have been in to look at the picture, and say it could not be more like. As I walk about the grounds, the laborers, old and young, lift their hats as I pass them. This respect and reverence sit but ill on me, who have been all the early part of life in as humble a sphere as those who pay it. What freak of fortune is this which has raised me from the hut in my native wilds to the table of a duke of the realm of Great Britain! By another freak, I may be sent back to the hovel again, but not to enjoy those innocent pleasures that were mixed with the toils of boyhood.

Sunday. Walked to Bothwell Brig; then to Bothwell Castle. The gardener showed me the gardens and hothouses, and the grounds, that are laid off most beautifully. We left this fertile spot for one calculated to awaken feelings of no ordinary nature. As we bent our course to the castle, we suddenly came into a full view of it, at about half a mile's distance from it, up the Clyde. It is strikingly beautiful as seen from this point. It stands upon a high bank, which has a frightful descent to the river below. One side of the castle is in tolerably good repair or preservation, but almost overgrown with ivy. The sun was bright, and there was not a breath to disturb the solemn silence that prevailed amidst these relics of ancient grandeur. One side of the castle has fallen to the ground; and large trees, at least a foot through, are growing on the heavy masses of stone, that were too strongly cemented to be broken. Larch-trees, two feet through, are now standing where the principal breach was made, like mighty conquerors viewing their fallen foe. The wall is about six feet thick, built of rough stone; and, wherever there are any crevices in it, vegetation is seen shooting forth. One who has not visited these or like ruins can form no idea of their sublimity. I sat down upon one of the stones that were formerly a part of this once impregnable fortress, and calmly viewed the surrounding walls. I thought of the thousands who had died in their defense: the same sun shone on them that now shines on me. They were as full of ambition as I am, and thought as little of this generation as I do of those yet unborn; and where are they now?

There is a finely built, showy, modern house standing within sight of these ruins; but it is only a dull reality: there is none of the poetry of association to make one pause to look at it a second time.

Sunday night. After dinner, took leave of the family. The duke urged me to stay a few days longer. The

91

duchess wished me every success, and Lord Archibald pressed me to call on him in London. The duke said if it was at any time in his power to serve me, he should be most happy to do so. He ordered a portrait of his Royal Highness, the Duke of Sussex. He advised me not to think of returning to my own country for the present. Thus ended a visit of ten days that I shall long remember with delight and gratitude, but no honor which a royal duke or any one else in this country can confer upon me will ever make me feel that pleasure which the remembrance of the kindness of the people of Boston has done.

Monday. Left the palace for Glasgow at nine o'clock.

Tuesday morning. Set off with Pattison and a small party of ladies for the Highlands: we crossed overland from Helensburgh to Loch Lomond, a distance of eight or nine miles. We got in sight of the loch about three o'clock; and, after taking our tea, we set off in a small row-boat for Ben Lomond, a distance of five miles. The day was fine. I wrote on the loch, in my pocket memorandum-book, 'In the middle of the loch, just as the sun is gilding the highest peaks of Ben Lomond. How heavenly the scene! The red clouds behind Ben Lomond look like fairyland, only more beautiful: all is still as the grave, save the plashing of the oars; the high mountains on either side are reflected in the crystal waters; the sun has just bid adieu to the highest rock of the mountain: no scene on earth can be more enchanting.' The loch is about four miles wide on an average, and very pure, cold water. We landed just at twilight, and entered a dirty Highland hut, called an inn, at the foot of Ben Lomond. Had my supper, and went to bed, but not to sleep; horrible beds, dirty sheets, and a very small room for two of us. We rose early, got a little breakfast, such as it was; and then five of us, Mr. P., Miss P., Miss Monteith, Miss Park, and myself, set off for the top of the mountain. The mountain is between three and four thousand feet above the loch: the manner in which we were obliged to wind our way up made a distance of about six miles to the top. The day proved fine, though we were occasionally enveloped in clouds that were scudding along the side of the hill. At last we reached the top, which was far above any clouds that were flying. What a singular sensation was produced by looking down upon the clouds! We amused ourselves with throwing down large stones. The hundred mountains in view, the lights and shades, the blue mist, and the most picturesque outline that can be formed, made the scene as heavenly as anything earthly can be.

We stayed on the hill an hour or two, and then descended. After a bad dinner, got on to a steamboat, and steamed down the loch. On our way to Dumbarton, we passed the house where Smollett was born. It stands on the beautiful river Severn, which is the outlet of the loch. The house is small and of no interest, except as having been the birthplace of this great man. Just op-

93

posite stands a small but neat monument to his memory. We arrived just before sunset at Dumbarton Castle; and, in order to see it, concluded to stay all night. The castle is kept by a governor and a few soldiers. It is said to be a miniature Gibraltar; it is a solid mass of rock; on the top is a spring of pure water. From it we had a charming view of the Clyde, both up and down.

Left Glasgow, Monday, August 30, for Stirling; went a part of the way in a canal-boat. Reached Stirling at four o'clock; very clear, fine weather. Went direct from the coach to the top of the castle, which affords one of the richest views I ever saw, except that from the top of Mount Holyoke, in Northampton. The Frith of Forth winds through a very fertile valley. The castle stands upon a rock one hundred and ninety feet above tide-water, and is in good repair, well garrisoned, with guns mounted. It looks to me impregnable.

Left at six next morning for Edinburgh, in a steam-boat; passed through a rich country. Arrived at the Black Bull at one o'clock. This is a splendid town of palaces, all of stone, and from five to ten stories high. Went through the castle of Edinburgh. Saw the crown of the Scottish kings: it is shown by lamplight, and seen through a strong iron cage such as lions and tigers are generally exhibited in. The castle is not unlike that at Stirling, strongly garrisoned. Went to see the new Bridewell; saw some poor condemned wretches at work on the tread-mill. Went to Holyrood House. This

94

Peter C. Brooks

is a splendid palace: the greater part of it is in perfect repair; the chapel is in beautiful ruin. In the centre of the chapel is the burying-ground of the Scotch nobility.

Thursday, September 2. Called upon Blackwood, and found him very civil. He said it was singular that Leslie, Newton, and myself should appear to him so soon after the article in his magazine giving so minutely the characteristics of each.

At four o'clock, left Edinburgh for Glasgow.

Sunday, September 5. Spent the day at Dunoon, a place opposite Gourock. In the course of the day, we took a boat, and rowed up the 'Holy Loch,' a beautiful sheet of water, surrounded on three sides by high and steep hills. At the foot of one of these stands the vault of the family of Argyll. It is situated in the centre of an old churchyard, with two platforms, about ten feet wide and two feet high, on which the coffins of many generations of the Argyll family lie. Some of the bodies are embalmed. The coffins are richly decorated with the arms of the family. I sat down upon one of these coffins, and could not help comparing the ashes that slept within with those of his vassals that lay unheeded in the yard without. The one was now as motionless as the other; the one was now as powerless as the other; the same grave had opened for both, and yet how different their lots in this world! There was something awfully solemn in this tabernacle of the dead. The faint light from one small window made even my com-

panions look like inhabitants of the place: we were glad
to return to the cheerful light of day.

Monday I returned to Glasgow.

Saturday, September 11. A call from J. S. Knowles
and Macready.

Saturday, September 18. We went over the grounds
of the Duke of Argyll. Saw a great many cypress and
yew trees, two of the former measuring eighteen feet in
circumference.

Monday, September 20. Returning this morning from
the Athenæum, I met a respectable merchant, and
asked, 'What news?' as carelessly as one asks 'Are all
well at home?' He replied, 'No news, no news at all. I
have been looking through the "Courier," and find nothing.' — 'But,' said I, 'did you not notice the death
of the two monarchs, Louis XVIII and Iturbide?' —
'Oh! yes, I saw that; but it will have no effect at all
upon trade.' This is a fair specimen of the trading class
of this great and populous city.

CHAPTER V

Wednesday, October 6, 1824. Made up my mind to
leave the city, and consequently settled with the landlady; received pay for my labors, and took an affection-
ate farewell of my friends. I got on to a steamboat at
ten o'clock, and sailed for Belfast, Ireland. This is a
fine town, containing about fifty thousand inhabitants.
Mr. Spurr, one of my fellow-travelers, agreed to go on
to Dublin with me; so we set off for that place in high
spirits. We passed through many very neat villages and
towns, much more so than the like towns in England
or Scotland; but they say this is the gem of the Emerald
Isle. The scenery in some parts is very fine.

We traveled over a great deal of the peat or turf
country. We passed by the Marquis of Cunningham's
seat, on the Boyne. The high cultivation, and the
beautiful little fall in the river, make this spot most
enviable. The river is about the size of the Deerfield
River. At seven o'clock, we arrived in the great city of
Dublin.

Saturday morning it set in to rain, and continued to
rain and blow a hurricane until Wednesday. I spent the
greater part of the day in calling upon the artists of
Dublin. I had a letter to Mr. Comerford, a protégé of
Mr. Stuart, who is the principal artist (a miniature
painter) in Ireland.

97

Tuesday, October 12. Still a most dreadful storm; accounts of many wrecks at Kingston and along the coast. Visited the public buildings. Dublin is a fine city, equal, if not superior, to Edinburgh. Yet it is a deserted town. How galling must it be to the feelings of a proud Irishman to see this decay of his nation's greatness! The splendid Parliament House is now converted into a banking-house; the mansions of their nobility are used as boarding-houses, hotels, etc.

Dined with Mr. Cummins, an amateur artist; a delightful party. In the morning, went with Mr. Comerford to Kingston, a distance of five miles, to see the effects of the gale. It was a horrible sight: wrecks in every quarter, some washing to pieces, some driven high and dry upon the sandy beach. In a new harbor just completed, which was thought very secure, there were four large ships broken to pieces. The new breakwater, a stupendous work of a mile in length with three railways upon it, was torn up by the heavy sea, not a vestige of the railways left; the stones were hove up like ice in a spring flood. While we were contemplating this scene, the waves having subsided a little so as to enable us to walk out on the ruinous pile, we saw a brig making for the harbor in distress. She had lost a part of her rigging, which rendered her in some degree unmanageable; and, besides, the crew, as we afterwards learned, were worn out with fatigue, so that she was unable to make the harbor, but was drifting fast upon the rocks, with a heavy sea and a strong wind to force her upon them. This was an awful moment: four or five hundred spectators within hail, yet unable to render the least assistance: it seemed that their doom was sealed. Their only reliance now rested upon the cable, which was literally their thread of life. The poor wretches had weathered the gale for fifty hours, and now so near land, and yet without a hope of escape! Many of the seamen, and two or three of the passengers, were clinging to the bulwarks of the ship to prevent their being washed off, unable to do more. At length a ray of hope beams upon them: a boat is discovered putting out from shore. It is a lifeboat, manned with twelve brave, stout tars. All eyes are now turned upon the half-worn-out cable. There is a universal cry of 'If it only holds until the boat comes up, they are safe!' This was the most painful and anxious moment of my life; hope and fear alternated in the breast of each beholder. Sometimes we heard the cry, 'She drags her anchor'; and then, 'No, she still holds'; until, at length, the boat came up and made fast under the lee of the brig; and the passengers and crew were seen crawling over the sides of the vessel, and letting loose their hold: we could see them fall like so many sacks into the boat. In a few moments more we had the pleasure of seeing these poor creatures snatched from what had seemed, so recently, inevitable destruction. Not long after this worn-out crew had left their perilous situation, another

99

boat was seen putting off from shore with as bold a crew as the former, but actuated by very different motives: they went to make a prize of the deserted wreck. At the imminent hazard of their lives, they succeeded in boarding and taking her away.

Here I had the mortification to see the frigate Essex, that had been taken during the last war, a prison hulk.

Wednesday, October 13. Left Dublin for Holyhead in the king's steam-packet. There was a tremendous sea rolling, in consequence of the late gale. Landed at Holyhead at two o'clock. Took a coach to Shrewsbury; slept at Bangor. At this place is now building a suspension bridge; the distance from one pier to another is five hundred and seventy feet, and very high: a ship under full sail can go under it.

Thursday morning at four we mounted our 'rolling world' and set off. When daylight came we were in full view of the Welsh mountains. They were beautiful, with the tops covered with snow. We wound our way through them for nearly thirty miles. The road is fine beyond conception (it was built by the government at an enormous expense), the hills are barren, rocky, and very steep. In every direction little streams as pure and white as snow are seen, tumbling down their sides. Now and then we meet a hut covered with green turf. On the very top of these lofty mountains is a small lake of pure, cold water, from which a little stream issues which increases rapidly, as it descends the mountain,

100

until it becomes a river. The Dee passes through a rich valley, highly improved. After leaving the Dee, the scenery is entirely uninteresting, and, like the greater part of England, to be admired for little else besides its cultivation.

Saturday, 16. Arrived safe in London. Called upon my friends and patrons, but found the most of them had left town. When I first arrived in London (in August, 1823), I was told that 'everybody was out of town.' I could not then understand it, but now I felt the truth of the remark. Spent a week in looking at the 'wonders.'

Sunday, October 17. Set off for the Duke of Norfolk's, at Fornham, Bury St. Edmunds. Arrived at three.

Monday morning, October 18. After breakfast, took a post-chaise to Fornham, a distance of two miles, for which I paid ten shillings. I had only paid twelve shillings from London to Bury. Cursed this imposition; but, as I was going to the duke's, it ill became me to complain. Arrived at the Hall at ten o'clock. Found his Grace with a small party at breakfast. He was very polite; introduced me to Sir Edward Codrington, Dr. Wollaston, and several other gentlemen. He was engaged for the day, so could not give me a sitting; but gave me a good horse, and introduced me to his factor. We rode all over the duke's grounds. In the course of the day, we went into the Court of Sessions. Nothing can be more ridiculous, in my estimation, than the

gowns and wigs of the lawyers. Heard some sharp dis-
putation, tinctured with sarcasm. I never heard so
much confusion in any of our pettifogging courts in
my life.

The duke lives in splendid style. Servants in every
direction to attend one's nod. The dukedom of Norfolk
is the finest in the realm.

Tuesday. Commenced the portrait; after which the
duke invited us all to ride with him over his farms. He
is a great agriculturist. His farms are as well conducted
as any in the country. His farmhouses are not only
comfortable, but would be called splendid in America.
Stables, barns, yards, etc., in the very best condition.
We returned about five to dress for dinner. The conversation of this circle is generally upon the 'sports of
the field,' or the 'turf,' the 'breed of hounds,' the 'pedi-
gree of a horse,' etc. Politics are seldom touched upon.
The variety of wines demands, of course, a share of
table-talk.

Thursday. Going on very well with the picture. Sir
Edward, I find, was at the battle of New Orleans, and
feels not a little sore on account of the rough reception
the British met with there.

Friday night, all hands went to the theatre at Bury.
The duke had 'ordered a play': so, after dinner, which
was early, we set off in two carriages. The theatre was
very much crowded; and, when *we* entered the box that
was appropriated to the duke, all eyes were turned upon

Mrs. Elizabeth Tuckerman Salisbury

us. Probably, for this once at any rate, I was taken for one of the great ones.

Monday, November 1. Finished the head of the duke. It is said by the company present to be the best portrait that has been taken of him. He has asked me to make a copy of it for him, and has promised to give me a sitting in town. He thinks I am mistaken in going back to America. He says America is too young for the arts to flourish.

Tuesday morning. Took leave of his Grace. He made many professions of friendship. He sent his carriage with me to Bury. As I approached the inn, I observed a good deal of bustle among the attendants and hangers-on. I soon guessed the reason. The duke's carriage could contain no ordinary personage. I waited for a short time, until the coach came up; and the first thing the landlord did was to whisper in the coachman's ear, who was remarkably civil during the journey.[1]

Wednesday evening, November 17. Left London for

[1] Mr. Harding often told a little incident which occurred upon this journey. His fellow-travelers, seeing him drive up in the duke's coach, took it for granted he was a man of rank; and, judging from his appearance that he was a military man, gave him the title of Colonel. They were very obsequious, and were so talkative, and used his imaginary title so frequently, that he grew weary of it, and, turning to them at last, said with some dignity, 'General, if you please.' But the higher his rank, the more persistent their attentions. At last the conversation turned upon America and American women, whom his companions depreciated in a way which aroused his indignation; and he warmly undertook their defense. They looked at him in surprise; and one at last remarked, 'You feel strongly about this matter.' 'And well I may,' was the reply; 'for I have an American woman for my wife, and an American woman for my mother.' After this he was troubled with no more superfluous attentions.

Dover, at which place we arrived at four P.M. As the boat left immediately for Calais, I could see nothing of the place. The boat had been detained two days by head winds blowing a gale. It was doubtful at first whether we should go or not; but the captain concluded to try it, and at ten we set off. I never experienced so disagreeable a motion in my life. The waves were rolling directly across our path, and our little boat was tossed about like an eggshell. Every soul on board, but the sailors, was sick. At three o'clock we made the port of Calais. Here, for the first time since I left home, I feel like a stranger. Everything that meets my eyes or ears is foreign. The appearance of the city and its inhabitants is strikingly different from anything that I ever met before. Calais is considered impregnable: it is a walled town. Great trouble and vexation at the custom-house.

Next morning we set off for Paris in a diligence. The English say a great deal of our bad roads and bad carriages; but they have only to cross the Channel to find, not only worse roads and worse coaches, but worse-looking establishments altogether. The horses are driven by rope lines — two wheel and three lead horses. The coachman rides postilion, and the horses jog on at the rate of about five miles an hour. As we traveled by night, we necessarily lost some of the views worth traveling for. We passed through two walled towns during the night, each of which I had a strong desire to see. The gates of each town were shut, and some little ceremony was necessary to get us through.

Saturday, November 20. Clear and cold. I rode by the side of the *conducteur* the greater part of the day; but, as he did not speak or understand one word of English, our conversation was very much confined to gesture. Nothing of especial interest during the day; passed some neat towns. At eight in the evening, we arrived in Paris, and stopped at the Hotel Meurice.

Sunday, November 21. After breakfast we set out in quest of wonders. The first thing we came upon was the Tuileries, then the gardens, then the Seine. The view from the toll-bridge is the most picturesque I have ever seen. I spend hours of the most exquisite delight in looking at this scene. The Louvre was open to the public, at least the new one; so we passed in without any difficulty. From what I had seen and read of the French artists, I was very much prejudiced against them; but to my delight, I found the *exposition* full of good pictures of every class, except portraits, and there were a few of those that were not bad. In the higher walks of art, they stand decidedly above the English. The English artists say the French are full of affectation; but I think there is as much affectation in the English, and of a less pardonable nature. A slovenly finish and a contempt for the minutiæ of nature seem to possess the English; while a love of the sublime, and a high finish, given even to the most trifling object, seem the ruling passion of the French. The latter have too much 'school,' while the former have too little. By far the greater part of the French pictures are of the highest school of art, while those of the English are of the lowest. Some of the large pictures in the present exhibition give me great delight; one in particular, by Cogniet, of Caius Marius on the ruins of Carthage. It is nearer perfection than any, either ancient or modern, that I have seen. It has poetry in every inch of it. The exhibition is full of beautiful interiors of cathedrals, convents, etc., and a great many in the style of Wilkie; but their portraits are, in general, wretchedly bad. There are two portraits by Sir Thomas Lawrence, which shine like diamonds among rubbish. Bowman and I joined in procuring some casts, and other materials for drawing.

After looking through the Louvre, we took a walk through the Tuileries gardens. Here is a sight that is worth a voyage across the Atlantic to see. Although the season of gayety has gone by, and the trees are leafless, yet the appearance to me was grand and enchanting. The fine groups of statues in marble, that one meets at every turn, are objects of no little interest to me. Although it was Sunday, we saw in the course of our walk several groups of children singing and dancing, while their parents and friends looked on with great interest. How different this is from the rigid Puritanism of the Scotch! Whether it be right or wrong, I will not attempt to say; but this much I must confess, it is innocent enjoyment to them, and conducive to good feeling between the children.

I am all impatience to get to painting again. I think I have benefited from looking at the French, as well as the antique, pictures. Am getting on a little in my French.

Wednesday, December 1. Dined with Mr. Brown. At six, Washington Irving, Mr. Bowdoin, Mr. Prince, and Mr. Finch called for me with a carriage. This did not look like a dinner 'without ceremony.' Not a little astonished to find eight or ten ladies assembled in the drawing-room. Had a sumptuous dinner, but rather stiff. I was seated by Lady Harvey, who is very affected in her manners. A ludicrous mistake occurred on the occasion of my making a ceremonious call upon Mr. Brown, after the dinner party. It was raining and very muddy; and, as I stood in the hall, wiping my feet, I said to the porter, by way of practicing my French, 'Il fait mauvais temps.' He respectfully replied, 'Oui, monsieur'; and immediately I heard 'Mons. Mauvais Temps' resounding up the stairway from one servant to another, to the great amusement of the party in the parlor, who, as soon as they saw me, comprehended the joke.

Last Saturday night, went to the Italian opera to see 'Othello.' The character of Desdemona, by Madame Pasta, was the most perfect thing possible: the character of Othello was also admirably played. Although

I could not understand the language, yet the music and gesture were so impressive that I could hardly contain myself. I could scarcely keep my seat during the last act: not a breath was heard from the audience during the performance. There is a charm in the Italian music which no other music possesses.

Went on Saturday to the Louvre. The French artists have more merit than I was at first disposed to give them. Their knowledge of anatomy is great: they draw well, and perhaps adhere as closely to nature as the English in point of color; yet they evince a want of taste in their choice. They generally choose the coldest light. But there is often a want of harmony about their pictures, as if their heads were painted in one light, the hands and drapery in another.

Tuesday, December 7. I went to see the grand library in Rue Richelieu: this is the finest establishment of the kind I have seen. Went also to see the model of the great elephant, commenced by Napoleon. This is about fifty feet high: it was to have been of bronze, and to serve as a fountain to supply the city, or a part of it, with water.

Wednesday, December 8. Bowman, Hayden, and myself set off for Versailles, which is twelve miles from the city. We first surveyed the grand palace, which is allowed by all to be the finest in the world. To go into a minute detail of all that I saw there, would be the work of a day. The palace has no furniture excepting pictures. The paintings were mostly done in the reign of Louis XIV, and much better than any the present age can produce. We then visited the Great and Little Trianon. The gardens of the latter are, I believe, thirty miles in circumference. The fountains are very numerous, and around each are allegorical figures.

Monday, December 13. Went with Bowman to view Père la Chaise, the common burying-ground of Catholic citizens of Paris. The most ordinary of the monuments has something tasteful, either in the workmanship of the stone or the decorations. Garlands of flowers are woven around the stones. This decorating the graves of departed friends is perhaps a weakness; yet it certainly is an amiable one, and can have no bad effect. On the contrary, it keeps alive that tender feeling of respect for the memory of those once loved, which all who live are so ready to hope for when they shall be numbered amongst the dead.

Tuesday, December 14. Determined to go to London this week. Went to see the celebrated painting in the dome of St. Geneviève Chapel, or, more commonly called, the Panthéon, by Baron du Bos (created by Charles X). It is a masterpiece of art, very difficult to execute; but, from the distance at which we were obliged to view it, it had a distorted and unnatural appearance.

Bowman and I now went to view the Louvre for the last time. We spent about three hours in the old gallery. I continue to like and dislike the same pictures I did at first, particularly the one I have before mentioned — of Marius. I never can pass it without feeling its superior worth — without paying adoration to it. It never fails to interest and give me pleasure.

Thursday, December 16. Set off for London. Landed at Dover at noon on Saturday. When the English custom-house officers came on board the steamer to inspect the baggage of the passengers, their suspicions fastened upon my friend Bowman. They searched his trunk thoroughly, and even his pockets; but found nothing contraband, and very little of anything else. Then came my turn. I had a quantity of gloves, and many other articles that were liable to seizure; but I gave them my key. They opened the trunk, looked at a few articles of dress which lay on top, and passed it. Bowman said to me, 'You were born to good luck.' He said it was my personal appearance which cleared me so easily, while it was his diminutive stature which aroused their suspicion of him. His personal appearance was certainly not much in his favor.

Sunday, December 19. Visited the cathedral at Canterbury. Wandered about in the long, echoing aisles in silent admiration. While we were wrapped in silence and thought, the grand organ began to chant. It carried me to sublimer regions. I never heard any music which seemed to inspire me with religion like this. It produced a pleasing, melancholy sensation, such

110

as I have felt in days long gone by, when under a grove of our native pines, listening to the hollow moaning of the breeze as it found its way through them.

Monday, December 20. Arrived in town last night, about eight.

Saturday, Christmas Day. This is a dull day with me; no one to go and take a family dinner with. The very preparation of others makes me unhappy. How foolish it is for me to live from home in the way I do! I think this is the last Christmas I will spend apart from my family.

TO C. M. H.

'LONDON, *December* 26, 1824

'. . . Mr. Williams has a portrait of his late mother by my old master Stuart; it is his last picture, and by no means his worst. I have invariably sounded his praise as an artist of the first distinction and merit, and it has as often been said by the artists and connoisseurs here, that my partiality to his pictures grew out of the respect I entertained for the man, and for the rank he held in America as an artist. But I have it in my power now to prove that my opinion is founded in reason and judgment. This picture, although Stuart was never highly thought of at home for his female portraits, is a masterly production, and will stand the test of a comparison with Sir Thomas, or any other living artist. I intend to have it exhibited this year, if possible, at Somerset House.'

111

CHESTER HARDING

'LONDON, *February* 12, 1825

'The article you speak of in "Blackwood" *was* written by John Neale. . . .

'The Duke of Sussex and Lady Anson continue to patronize me as warmly as ever. This is very gratifying to my feelings. I breakfast and dine with them very often. I am painting a large half-length for the Duke of Hamilton. I feel that my improvement is great within the last nine months. My visit to Paris was of great service to me; I saw a great deal in the way of art that was excellent, as well among the moderns as the ancients, and although I did not paint while I was there, yet I profited by the viewing of these excellent models.

'My dear fellow, I am living within two doors of the house where the immortal Reynolds lived and died. Who knows but there may be some magic in the atmosphere around the hallowed spot? If so, perchance *I* may inhale it, and like him cause my canvas to breathe — ahem! — My modesty won't allow me to say more, nor even read what I have written. I pay enormously high for my rooms, $75 per month. This is a high go, but "neck or nothing" with me, you know. The situation and light are good.'

Friday, February 18. The season of gayety is fast approaching; but, beyond my profession, what does it

112

Alexander Hamilton Douglas, Tenth Duke of Hamilton
Painted in 1825 at his country seat, Lanarkshire, Scotland

signify to me? Perhaps I may be invited now and then to a dinner; but it is very annoying frequently, when there is no annoyance meant. To get into a hackney-coach full of dirt and straw, with one's very best fix-up on, with silk stockings and white kid gloves, and start off to a dinner, and arrive, perhaps, just as my Lord's carriage and turnout are setting down, with, perhaps, my Lady So-or-so waiting her turn, and wondering what that vulgar man was invited for to intercept her passage, is rather galling to one's pride, although he be a republican born and bred. This is a good sort of place enough for a man of wealth and leisure. He will always find amusement of some kind; and if he wish to become fashionable, in the high sense of the word, this is his place. But for a man who has to depend upon his hands for his bread, whose very time is his money, particularly if his profession be of an intellectual nature, it is no place. A man in any profession that requires mental exertion is kept alive by the cheering applause of his friends. He needs constant encouragement from them; it is the food of genius. Without it, his efforts dwindle into mere mechanical drudgery.

> 'Ah! who can tell how hard it is to climb
> The steep where Fame's proud temple shines afar?
> Ah! who can tell how many a soul sublime
> Hath felt the influence of malignant star,
> And waged with fortune an eternal war;
> Checked by the scoff of pride, by envy's frown,

And poverty's unconquerable bar,
  In life's low vale, remote, hath pined alone,
  Then dropped into the grave, unpitied and unknown?'

Sunday, February 27. Two months of my rent have gone up, and I have not done enough to pay it and my other expenses; but I hope for better times.

The duke sat on Thursday last, and was very pleasant, and seemed delighted with the picture. He thinks I have made wonderful progress in the art since I first painted him. So I have; but he is as much pleased with the flattery in the last picture as he is with my improvement. There is not a human being on earth who is not susceptible to flattery; and he who flatters most in this great city will do the most judicious thing.

Tuesday. Sent the duke and Mr. Atkinson to the exhibition in Suffolk Street.

Friday. Dined with Mr. Smith. In almost all the dinner-parties in high life that I have attended, I have seen very little ease or enjoyment of anything beyond the bottle and the dinner. The company, with one or two exceptions, are exceedingly on their guard, measuring their sentences with great care, and laughing very mechanically. My impressions, however, may be influenced by my own want of ease and enjoyment.

While we were at the table, after the ladies had retired, we separated into knots, some talking upon political economy, some upon religion, some upon politics. I overheard one man, who was a member of Parliament, say that it was believed the United States would soon be divided into two or more separate governments; that the presidential election would be the great cause. This he urged against universal suffrage. But as I was not of his little squad, I did not say aught to the contrary, nor even pretend to listen to him: he did not know I was an American.

Monday, April 4. The exhibition in Suffolk Street is opened. There are some good pictures; but the balance is so much against them that they appear but indifferently.

Bowman had sent two pictures to this exhibition; and, like myself, not doubting but they would find a good situation in the best room, had not taken the trouble to inquire after them. On my first entering the rooms, I looked about, but saw none of his in the little room. Well, thought I, he is at least in the large room, whether they have given him a good light or not; so on I pushed, and soon encountered my own two portraits in a capital light. Now for Friend Bowman! I looked about, but saw him not; I looked again, and was again disappointed. Is it possible, thought I, that they have rejected him? My suspicions were soon confirmed: they had sent his pictures back to him without the least explanation. Now one of the most painful offices devolved upon me a man can have to perform. I had promised to see Bowman that night, and tell him how his pictures looked, what sort of light they were hung in, etc. The hearing the fate of his pictures gave him, I believe, less pain than the telling him of it did me.

Having made up my mind to an excursion to Glasgow, I gave Bowman the use of my lodgings, and set off by the coach immediately. Passed through Dumfries. This is where the mortal remains of 'Nature's sweetest poet' lie buried. The coach stopped but for twenty-five minutes, the usual time allowed to passengers for refreshment. This time, short as it was, I preferred to spend in feasting my mind and imagination. The churchyard was at least three minutes' walk, or, I should say, run, from the inn; for I went with such speed through the streets as to astonish the good people I met. When I arrived at the churchyard, I found an old woman ready to let me in at once, and I lost no time in letting her know that I preferred looking about me to her prating; by which means I was shown at once to the spot I had so longed to see. This was consecrated ground, where I was disposed to linger, and forget all earthly things in the contemplation of the heavenly part of him who lay entombed beneath my feet. The monument is simple and beautiful, and the death-like stillness of everything about me led me into a delightful train of thought. While I was lost to everything external, I heard the grating sound of a horn, the discordant effect of which sent a chill through my veins. I wished that confounded horn and its owner to the dogs. But it was fortunate for me that I heard it; for it proved to be the bugle of the guard, who was summoning the passengers to their seats. So, after being fairly brought to myself again, I looked at my watch, and found that I had stayed the full length of my allotted time; and it was only by the same speed I made in going to, that I made in going from, the inn that I reached it before the coach left.

On this journey, I met with an amusing instance of sycophancy. The day before I arrived in Glasgow, I had the misfortune to fall in with a title-worshiper, and was obliged to ride by his side all day. In the course of the day, an officer got on the seat with the driver, which led this companion of mine to turn his attention considerably towards him. He was conjecturing the probable rank of the officer, when I happened to espy a sword-case, marked Captain Sir Something, which I pointed out to my friend. The moment he saw it, he ejaculated in broad Scotch, 'My God! he's a nobleman.' This was enough for Sawney. Now how to ingratiate himself with the nobleman was his only care. He, however, being richly endowed with the sagacity for which his countrymen are so noted, soon hit upon the surest means of effecting his object. He flattered the officer; laughed at all his stale jokes; was, in short, everything the nobleman could have wished. At dinner, there was a good opportunity to show off, and the Scotchman took advantage of it. He teased him to death by pressing him to take this or that. He was, at least, a bore to all

117

but the officer. The time at length arrived when the 'nobleman' was to take his leave of us. I will not attempt to describe the chagrin the poor Scotchman evinced when he found the man had gone — but the sword-case was left behind! All he could say was, 'My God! and he's no nobleman after a'.'

TO C. M. H.

GLASGOW, *April* 14, 1825

'You will no doubt be a good deal surprised to find that I am again in the "land o' cakes." It was one of my sudden moves. I made up my mind upon the subject within the space of ten minutes after the thing first occurred to me. You will recollect that I painted a few heads when I was here last autumn. They gave so much satisfaction that I was invited by several of the friends of those that I painted to return to Glasgow, at the same time accompanying the request with the promise of several pictures. It certainly was not the proper time to leave London, but the fine weather and the probability of my being rather idle until after the opening of Somerset House, together with the love of the root of all evil, had their influence, and I was not long in determining to set off. I arrived here on Saturday last. I have been here but three days, have got rooms, and commenced pictures to the amount of $600, and shall begin another to-morrow, which certainly augurs well. It is most gratifying to know that my pictures are approved of after a six months' contemplation. Not infrequently the interest in a picture wears off with its novelty, but it seems quite the reverse with those I left in Glasgow.'

April 7, took up my abode with Walter in Buchanan Street. In the course of six weeks I realized £350.

During this short but profitable visit, I received great attention from several of the first families in the place. My friends, the Messrs. Pattison, were unceasing in their attentions. Professor Davidson and others were also very kind. I was invited to a dinner given by the college club to Mr. Dunn. Here I was placed in an embarrassing situation. The company, to the number of twenty-four, were very merry; toasting the college club, the corporation of Glasgow, and many other public institutions, when Mr. Davidson rose, and proposed as a toast, 'Success to the fine arts, and the health of Mr. Harding.' This, coming so unexpectedly, threw me completely off my balance. I, however, thanked them for the honorable mention they had been pleased to make of me. Pretty soon, the president of the college, a reverend doctor, began a long speech by saying that, until that moment, he did not know that they had the honor of a distinguished artist and a foreigner at their dinner. He concluded by proposing more directly, 'The health of Mr. Harding.' Then followed a round of applause. This was ten times more embarrassing than the former; and I could only say 'that I felt most sensibly the honor they had done me, and begged to return them my sincere thanks.' I thought, when the venerable doctor had concluded his eloquent speech, that I would attempt to address the company, and say something more than merely 'Thank ye'; but the solemnity of rising disconcerted me so much that I hardly knew whether I spoke or only whispered.

Many portraits are partly promised, in case I should return.

It was during this visit that I made up my mind to send for my family, and make Glasgow my home.

Now, being very anxious to see the exhibitions in London, I closed my engagements here, and set off again for that city. I took barely money enough to pay my way on the most economical basis; but, as I have never yet learned to act upon that basis, I got myself into a sad dilemma. At Nottingham, I had to pay my fare to London, which was just two pounds; but, as I was reduced to just that sum, I should have no change for refreshments, or for the guard and coachman. So I paid one pound, and left the other to be paid on my arrival in town. I got on very well until we arrived at the mail-stage office in Islington: here I got off the coach, and ordered my portmanteau into the inn, and went to the bar, and asked the landlady to let me have a pound, at which she seemed somewhat astonished; nor would she comply with my request until the guard became responsible to her for that sum, although she had my trunk. I got the pound at last, and paid the remainder of my fare; and the coach drove off to the merry notes of the bugle.

I went to the bar, and asked the bar-maid to show me my room; but, lo! I could get no bed at all, as she said they were full. Here was a pretty business — my trunk in pawn, no money, and not a very prepossessing appearance, as I had not shaved, nor changed my linen, for three days. I, however, set off in quest of another inn, though the idea of again exposing myself to the scrutinizing gaze of that beggarly race of waiters was not the most pleasant. But there was no alternative; so I bolted into the bar of the Angel Inn, with, as I thought, a confident manner, and asked the head-waiter to give me a bed. 'Directly, sir.' 'But,' said I, 'you will oblige me, if you will let me have a pound to redeem my portmanteau.' The waiter looked very cautiously at me, but, after some hesitation, called the 'boots,' and said, 'Here, take this pound, and go with the gentleman, and pay for his trunk, and bring it here.' As soon as we arrived at the inn again, I called for pen, ink, and paper; at which brief demand they all seemed to stare with great amazement. They obeyed, however, and I was soon shown into my room. When I called for the writing materials, I thought I would write a line to Mr. Williams, but changed my mind, and went to bed.

I had not been there many minutes before I heard stocking-feet steps at or near my door, and I soon guessed at their object. I could hear them say, 'Oh! he's gone to bed.' The next morning, a servant came early into my room with, 'Did you ring, sir?' but evidently to see if I had not made way with myself; and really, when I came to look at myself by daylight, in the glass, I did not so much wonder at their suspicions. I was shockingly sunburnt, with a long beard, and altogether a frightful object. Before I went down, however, I shaved, and put on some clean linen. The good folks of the inn no longer stared at me, but were rather civil, particularly after I had returned from Mr. Williams, with my hands full of banknotes.

I now took a coach for my lodgings. During my absence, Bowman had collected almost all the pictures he had painted in England, and strewed them about the rooms; and had left them to their fate. He was in such despair that he kept aloof from all respectable society.

I set off directly for the Somerset House. As it had opened during my absence, I felt the greatest impatience to see the paintings. I did not feel that degree of anxiety about my own pictures that I did the year before, as I knew where they were placed; still I was very desirous to see how they stood the comparison with other pictures. I was happy to think that they were among the *best*, not the worst, class in the exhibition. I must say that I looked at them with as much, and perhaps the same kind of, pride as a mother feels in looking at her beautiful daughter on her presentation at court. It filled me with laudable ambition to excel; but I can here solemnly aver, that envy or jealousy of any other artist's talents or eminence never entered into my mind. I never felt a greater pleasure in my profession than then. It is a noble art, thought I; it is, of all others in the world, the most delightful. But here the thought of my friend Bowman broke in upon my delight. Poor fellow! he had sent four pictures to Somerset House — the two that were rejected at Suffolk Street and two new ones; but, sad to relate, they were all condemned as unworthy a place. This was certainly a disagreeable shade in the delightful pictures I had just been drawing of the profession. Here was Bowman, by two years my senior in the art, and who had ever since his commencement been flattered, and taught to believe that he was a wonderful genius; and now, after eight or nine years of hard study, his hopes are blasted in this cruel manner. I sat upon a bench for — God knows how long, looking into vacancy, and thinking painfully of the discouragements of the artist. I made up my mind that he too was not free from perplexities.

My absence from London, though short, had, I found, broken up my connections in a great degree. Some of my friends (I should say patrons) were about leaving town. Others had much to say of the gayeties of the past season; of their thankfulness that it was

over; of their wretched, haggard faces, and similar subjects, unfavorable to that branch of the fine arts which
depends mainly upon the vanity of mankind for its
support. So I concluded to spend a few weeks looking
at the works of art, and then return to Glasgow.

August 9. Left London, with all my implements of
painting. This was not effected without some regret.
London never looked more charming than it did just
then, although everybody was out of town. The idea
of bidding it adieu, perhaps an eternal one, was painful.
I don't know how it is, but I feel a great attachment to
the great metropolis, inhospitable as it is. It is the
fountain-head of everything that is excellent in my profession, as well as every means of attaining excellence
in it. But I took my seat on the top of a coach; and, in
the noisy bustle about the coach-office, and the amusing variety one always meets with on such occasions, I
set off in very good spirits.

Safely arrived in Glasgow, I began the arduous task
of finding apartments. I then collected a few of my old
pictures, which, added to those I had brought down
from London, made a tolerable exhibition. But work
was slow to come. Day after day I spent in contemplating my beautiful light, which I had been at six pounds'
expense in cutting out of the roof. I found some relief,
however, in furnishing my house, in expectation of the
arrival of my family. Before I left Glasgow for London,
while I was very busy, dozens were talking of sitting,

124

Judge Samuel F. Lyman

and three positively agreed to sit on my return; but I find they have changed their mind. Should I again be pressed with more than I can attend to, no doubt they will be as anxious as at first to have their pictures taken. How fickle are people of quality, as they consider themselves, in regard to matters of taste!

TO S. F. L.

' 29 MILLER STREET, GLASGOW, *October*, 1825

'DEAR LYMAN — I now sit down to acknowledge the receipt of my wife and children, who came safe to hand on the 24th of September. After I had come to the determination to send for them, I was very impatient for their arrival. I thought more about them in the two months' interval between my first decision and their arrival than I had in the whole two years previous; for while I was passing the allotted time of probation in my pursuit of professional knowledge, I did not allow myself to think of my family as a treasure to be enjoyed until the expiration of my two years, therefore it had become to me a dream of future happiness, like fortune or renown, a something that was to be the reward of voluntary exile. But after having determined upon their coming out, and more particularly after receiving a letter in reply to my invitation, I was all impatience. I began first to count the weeks, and then the days, and then the hours that separated us.'

I received a letter from my wife, on her arrival at

Liverpool, telling me of her safe voyage, and her intended departure from Liverpool on the steamboat City of Glasgow; so, on my arrival at Greenock, I began to look for the boat, and soon had the delight of seeing her. My impatience to know if my family were on board was almost beyond control. A few revolutions of the heavy wheels brought us alongside of the object my eyes had been, for the last hour, so steadily riveted upon. I then saw my wife, and waved my hand to her; but we kept out of speaking distance for some time. During this short interval, the risible muscles of my face became excessively painful, from the great effort it cost me to suppress a downright schoolboy laugh.

Then came the meeting — then followed ten thousand inquiries after one and another, in such rapid succession that one could not be answered before another was asked. We directly went aboard a Glasgow boat, and in three hours arrived in safety at my own lodgings.

I now took up my abode in Glasgow, with my family around me; and should have been perfectly happy, if I could have seen my way clear for gaining a support for them. I had no work on hand, and the trade of the community was seriously depressed, while there was little prospect of any immediate renewal; so that I sometimes wished I had gone to, instead of sending for, my family. Fortunately for me, several of my friends interested themselves in my behalf, and got for me an order to paint a full-length portrait of the 'Deacon Convener of

Trades,' who was a very popular man. I was successful in my work, and exhibited with *éclat*. This brought me many sitters: indeed, for five or six months I was kept constantly employed.

I painted many of my best pictures at this time; but I found as my anxieties for my family increased, my enthusiasm for my art decreased. At times I felt a strong desire to go to Italy; but how could I leave my wife and four children? Sir Joshua Reynolds was right when he said a painter's wife or mistress should be his lay-figure, and his art should be his first and only love.

The summer following (1826) was the most disastrous to all branches of business that had ever been known in the kingdom. Nearly every country bank failed; and a universal panic seized the public mind, spreading through all classes of society. I was out of business: no one wanted pictures while this excitement lasted, and no one could tell when it would end. I thought seriously of returning to America, and consulted the Duke of Hamilton about my plans. He at first favored my going to Edinburgh; but, after weighing all the circumstances, he finally agreed that I was right, telling me I could return when the condition of the country was more prosperous.[1] This interview settled the question. I finished what pictures I had on the easel, collected

[1] In a farewell letter to Mr. Harding, the Duke of Hamilton writes: 'Nature with an indulgent hand has given you much; much you have acquired by your own labor and industry, and I shall rejoice to learn that genius and assiduity have been deservedly remunerated.'

what money was due me, and left Glasgow for Liverpool.

I had to take leave of many good and true friends, which was a sore trial: among them were James Sheridan Knowles, John Pattison — one of nature's noblemen — and many others, all of whom wished me Godspeed.

This step was not taken without the most painful regrets. No artist had a fairer prospect of rising to the highest rank in his profession, with such patrons as the Dukes of Sussex and Hamilton, and many other influential persons; and with Lady Anson's unwavering friendship. But I could not live through the universal prostration of business. I was influenced in my decision even more by another consideration. I had three daughters, nine, seven, and three years old. They were very pretty. Should they, when they grew up, fulfill the promise of their childhood, I felt they would be exposed to dangers growing out of the state of society in England which they would be free from at home. My profession entitled me to move in the highest circles, in which, at the same time, my wife and children would not be recognized. This is one of the cruel customs of the aristocracy of Great Britain.

We were weather-bound in Liverpool; but the impatience that I naturally felt at my compulsory stay was much alleviated by the kindness of Mr. Roscoe, whose acquaintance I made through a letter from the Duke of Hamilton. He was very kind and attentive, and

128

*Mrs. Johnson, Wife of a Boston Physician;
formerly a Miss Claggett, of Maryland*
Painted about 1826

showed me everything that was of any interest in the city. Among other things, he took me to see Mr. Audubon's collection of birds, which he had just brought with him from America. I saw all the original paintings, and very beautiful they were.

After two weeks' weary watching of the weathercock, the wind changed at last, and we put out to sea about the first of September.

No pen can describe the pleasure we felt when, after an uncomfortable passage of forty days, we sailed into Boston harbor.

It was Sunday; and with a fair, light breeze and bright sun, the scene was enchanting. All the annoyances of the voyage were forgotten: seasickness and head-winds were as though they had not been. As I took a parting look at the good ship Topaz, I could not but feel grateful to her, as though she had been 'a thing of life,' for the part she had taken in bringing us through so many storms. Her ultimate fate cost me a sigh, when I heard of it. Her next voyage was to India, where she was captured and burnt by pirates.

After reeling about awhile on the wharf, a store or counting-room was opened; and we staggered up a long flight of stairs, like so many intoxicated persons. We took a carriage, and drove to the Exchange Hotel. What a luxury it was to sit down to dinner, and find the dishes and tumblers keep their places!

I walked out with the children. Everything had a

CHESTER HARDING

diminutive appearance. The Common was not what it used to be in old times. The children took but little interest in what they saw; but they had one wonder to tell their mother of, that they had not seen a *single beggar*. I met many old friends, who gave me a hearty welcome home.

TO CHESTER HARDING

ON HIS DEPARTURE FROM BRITAIN FOR AMERICA

Son of another shore! We bid thee not
To linger longer in this alien land —
Alien in nought but distance — while thy thought,
Anticipating Time, doth to the strand
Of thy far Father-home waft thee away:
Ours be the fond farewells that say not 'Stay!'
But 'tis because we love the *World's Young Hope*,
Thy country, more than even we love thee,
That we do seek not to transplant a lop
From her yet budding boughs of Art's green tree
Into our earth, though yet we trust it drew
Some healthful nurture from our older soil.
No, Harding, no — of such she yet hath few:
Go — and enrich her with triumphant toil!

JAMES SHERIDAN KNOWLES

July, 1826

CHAPTER VI

Upon his return from Scotland Mr. Harding's family spent a few months in Northampton, Massachusetts, among their old friends, and then rejoined him in Boston. Upon their arrival he writes to his friend S. F. Lyman:

'Boston, *February* 8, 1827

'My dear Lyman — On Thursday, the first instant, I received my wife and children, all in good condition. I had a lodging provided where I took them on the night of their arrival. I was not the only one delighted by this event; the children were frantic with delight: they laughed and cried and chattered like magpies. I am now a good, steady, fatherly old man once more, and I can assure you that I am much happier in all respects than before.

'As to financial matters, my dear friend, I can say that I am doing tolerably well. Since I commenced I have painted to the amount of $1400, and I have little doubt that my business will increase rather than diminish. I find my pictures give satisfaction, and if I am not gaining popularity to the degree that I did when I was here before, I feel that I am gaining fame, which is a thousand times preferable. It is rather against me that I created such an excitement then — an interest

131

that could not by any human exertion be kept alive. I am identified with my former pictures, and as they are not worthy the high encomiums that were passed upon them, the natural consequence is a reaction, which I have to contend with; but perseverance will do wonders.

'My dear fellow, I have bid adieu to Northampton for a while. My present plan is to buy a house in Boston, and run the risk of paying for it by and by. Mr. Solicitor Davis says that the only money he is worth was made by being in debt. He therefore recommended to me the same course.

'Why don't you visit the great seat of learning this winter? Come down while Macready is here. He is expected soon.'

TO S. F. L.

'AT HOME, No. 9 CEDAR STREET

'. . . You will perhaps want to know how much rent I pay. I have taken a house for two years at $400 per year, with the privilege of vacating it at the expiration of one, by paying twenty-five dollars extra. We are within a stone's throw of the Misses Cabot, and very near Mrs. Eliot and Mrs. Minot, all of whom are pleasant neighbors, you know.

'I am happy to tell you that my professional labors have increased rather than otherwise, and that, in spite of the cost of furnishing, I have still a little left to feed upon in case of a "rainy day."

Leverett Saltonstall

'I have written to Mr. Hale of Quebec to let him know that if he is still desirous that I should visit his ancient city I will do so.'

TO S. F. L.

'MONTREAL, *June* 24, 1827

'It is not long since you had a line from me dated Boston, informing you of my intention of visiting H.M. dominions, in the hope of combining profit and pleasure; but how far I shall realize either I am not prepared to say. I must confess, however, that the pleasure of traveling in this province is not so unalloyed as that of traveling through the mother country. I have met with more arrogance, illiberality, and willful error on all subjects relative to the States, in the short time that I have been here, than I met with during my three years' visit in England. Not to speak of the luxury of good roads, good carriages, and good accommodation at inns, etc., there is nothing to be seen of improvement in agriculture, nor in any of the fine or useful arts. The farms are miserably tilled, the dwellings are inconvenient, with bad out-houses, if any at all; and this want of thrift pervades almost all classes of farmers, Canadian as well as Europeans. I see no hope of its becoming better under the present subjection to the mother country. If you are in company with an Englishman, no matter what his pretensions may be, he is always talking of home—"We do these things differ-

133

ently at home." Not a single individual have I met who does not consider himself in a state of temporary exile; they don't care a straw what becomes of the country if they get their ends answered. No man cares about internal improvements, no individual, I should say, for certainly the crown is expending some thousands yearly on canals and fortifications, and the only interest the individuals resident here seem to take in the disbursements is in securing to themselves a large share of the money. Now I hold this state of things to be incompatible with a thriving and well-founded government.

'I have spent a week with my old comrade B——, who lives about twenty miles above the city. He has bought a farm of eighty acres and is wasting some money in improvements upon it. It would baffle the skill of a veteran farmer to bring it into anything like a thriving or wholesome state. It is completely overrun with thistles, and besides, the Canadians have no conception of renovating land by manure. Their system is to cart the manure that is made in their barn-yards, on the ice, before the river breaks up in the spring, that it may be washed out of the way. After such a practice for a hundred years, what can you expect of a farm?

'What a stupendous river the St. Lawrence is! If its banks were peopled by an independent and enterprising population, there would be no counting the wealth that would flow down upon its surface. There would soon be canals large enough for steamboats to pass from the Gulf of St. Lawrence to Lake Ontario. But, alas, it is doomed for many years to come to see no larger barks than her canoes pass over her gentle rapids. . . .

'There is but one subject that the heterogeneous mass of English, Irish, Scotch, and French agree upon, and that is in most cordially hating the Yankees. . . .'

TO S. F. L.

'No. 16 BEACON STREET, BOSTON, *December*, 1827

'. . . The truth is, I have been too much absorbed in the man of business to think of sitting down to devote an hour exclusively to writing a letter. I have not got the deed yet, but I have had possession of my new house on Beacon Street for five weeks past, and am about moving into it with my family.[1] The room that I have fitted up is the finest in the world for my *trade*, and with the alterations and improvements that I have made, the family part is by no means contemptible. I have painted the front, which makes a great change for the better. . . .

'As to the sum over and above the $6500 to be secured by mortgage, I have borrowed $1000 on short credit, and I believe that I can muster the rest without great inconvenience from my outstanding debts. . . .

'Although I have been so much taken off the *shop*, in playing the man of business, I have done several por-

[1] This house is still standing, and is now occupied by the Unitarian Society. Some additions to the front were made about 1885. Horace Harding, father of the reviser of this book, was born there in 1828.

traits, one in particular of Mrs. Daniel Webster, which has elicited from her husband a voluntary promise that he will sit to me the moment he returns from this political campaign.'

'BALTIMORE, *May 6*, 1828

'... You know, of course, that I have been leading a vagabond life for the last three or four months, three of which I spent in the great city of Washington; but you may not know that for the last three months my health has been but indifferently good. Indeed, some of the time I have been as miserable a devil as ever was afflicted with that most miserable complaint, the dyspepsia. I am in hopes of mastering it by rigid discipline. I am convinced that the disorder has been growing upon me for the last eight months. It acts upon the intellectual as well as the animal man. It is the cause of the "blue devils" and similar diseases of the mind. I think if I were in Northampton, where I could take a great deal of horseback exercise and breathe the pure Yankee air once more, that I should soon be myself again. It may, however, be some weeks yet before I leave this city, at least I should like to paint a few more heads. In short, I want to get out of debt, and then I should be easy.

'My visit to Washington, notwithstanding my indisposition, has been one of profit and pleasure. I have had

136

Chester Harding
Self-portrait painted about 1828

the gratification of seeing a good deal of the great men of the age, particularly Judge Marshall. I am convinced that I shall feel through life that the opportunity to paint the Chief Justice, and at the same time hear him converse, would be ample compensation for my trouble in accomplishing these objects. But over and above all that, I have got portraits of *all* the Supreme Judges. I am busy in this place, although there is a tremendous stagnation in the commercial world. They are looking, however, with great hopes to the completion of the Chesapeake and Ohio Railroad (Baltimore and Ohio Railroad), but it won't do; the place is already overgrown, with a wretchedly poor country back of it.'

TO A YOUNG ARTIST

'RICHMOND, *October* 14, 1829

'Yours of the 28th of September I received a few days since, and I now sit down with pleasure to reply to it. In the first place, on the subject of your peregrinations. I think I may say with a good deal of certainty that you would meet with encouragement enough in the western world to defray expenses, and I think a good deal more. However, times are bearing heavily on all parts of the country and upon all classes of men; at least so I find it here. I think you would be as likely to do well in some of our country towns in New England, say Montpelier, the capital of Vermont, Burlington, or some of the towns in New Hampshire. But I would advise your charging so low that the cost of a picture need not stand in the way of your getting sitters, as it is not money you want so much as practice, for a year or two. Therefore I would paint for twenty-five dollars, though it is a little humiliating.

'That there are, as —— says, a multitude of starving artists, I make no doubt; but I do doubt what his murmurings would imply, that taste in England is on the wane. He is subject to seasons of despondency like all men of ardent temperament. When once a man begins to receive praise for his works, it is no longer possible for him to live without a constant stream of it. If it is stopped or turned for a time to some other quarter, he thinks that he is forsaken or neglected — begins to curse his hard fate, and, without the least philosophy, often gives himself up to the most gloomy forebodings.

'In our art, and I suppose in that of sculpture too, the first steps are easily taken, and not only the artist, but all his friends look upon the first dawnings of genius with the most enthusiastic admiration. They say, and he believes, that he is to outstrip everybody who is on the stage before him. He is cheered while yet on the threshold by his own advance. But he soon finds, as he is beginning to grope his way by some shorter way than others have taken who have preceded him, that difficulties arise on all sides. By and by he begins to wish that he had taken the surer, though beaten track, pointed out by so many who have gone before him.

138

His friends, too, begin to be impatient of his slackened pace, and gradually grow cool in their zeal; from coolness they go to indifference, next, to neglect. Now if the young man has the heart to go on in search of truth and fame, he is no ordinary genius, and is sure to reap the reward ultimately. What is more often the case, however, is that he is totally disheartened, regards his profession no longer with enthusiasm, but merely as a means of getting bread, and if in that light it offers greater rewards for his daily labor than the trade he gave up, he pursues it, if not, he goes to the "last," or strikes out some new line of industry. Now our friend, although a sensible man, is likely to be a little elated by the success with which his début has been marked, and consequently is likely to be depressed in the same ratio for a time. His is a genius that will ultimately soar above all ordinary obstacles, I may say imaginary obstacles, for there are, in fact, but few that are real. Once we begin to allow trifles to affect us, there is no end to the evils that we shall be sure to meet with on every side; at least, I find upon examination that nine tenths of my perplexities are but imaginary.'

Following his return from England, Mr. Harding's narrative continues:

I now began my career again in Boston; not as I did on my first appearance in that city, for then I was entirely self-taught, and little could be expected of one

139

from the back-woods: but now I came fresh from the schools of Europe, and with some reputation. I felt keenly how much more would be required of me, to fill the expectations of the connoisseurs and patrons of art.

My first picture was of Emily Marshall, then the reigning beauty of Boston. No artist's skill could be put to a severer test; for her beauty depended much upon the expression of her animated face, which, when lighted up in conversation, was bewitchingly lovely. I did not succeed to my own satisfaction, though others seemed well pleased.[1]

Much interest was shown in my paintings, and I soon had enough to do; though, of the eighty applicants on my list when I left Boston, not one came to renew his engagement. Many whom I had painted previously wanted their pictures altered, either because the dress

[1] The following passage is taken from a letter from Miss E. S. Quincy of Quincy, Massachusetts, to one of Mr. Harding's children:

'How well I remember both his studios. The first was in Beacon Street, near the present Athenæum, — I can see the portraits ranged on the floor, for they succeeded each other so rapidly there was no time to frame and hang them. His second studio was in Cornhill, and I can see the portraits of Emily Marshall, and of Mrs. Webster, in the dress she wore at Bunker Hill on the day of the celebration, June 17, 1825, — a pearl-colored hat and pelisse. It was impossible, as your father says, to catch the living fascination of Emily Marshall's face — but his portrait, I am told, is the only record which remains of her beauty. She was the most celebrated belle who ever appeared in our country, and was as much admired by ladies as by gentlemen, and although she was ever before the public, as it were, her celebrity never waned. If she walked in the street, I always expected a smile and a bow from her, and never passed her father's house without looking up to see her beautiful face brought out in full relief against the crimson curtain.'

Emily Marshall, Famous Boston Beauty
Painted about 1826

was out of fashion, or the expression did not please them, etc.; but I found it would never do to begin to alter the old pictures. So I adopted for a rule, that I would paint a new picture in the place of the old one, and deduct the price of the latter. I now charged one hundred dollars for a head: my former price was fifty dollars.

Among the sitters I had at this time was Timothy Pickering of Salem. He was far advanced in years, but as bright in intellect as a man of thirty. His conversation was extremely interesting, though it mostly pertained to the early days of our government. One day, I felt a strong desire to know how a man would feel who knew that his allotted time was nearly spent, and thought I might venture to put the question to him; so I said, 'You have lived beyond the average of human life: how do you feel upon the subject of the final departure to the other world?' His reply was, 'It was only the other day I was asking old Dr. Holyoke the same question.' The doctor was some ten years his senior.

I had at this time, to take care of my room, a boy who afforded me much amusement. I came into my studio one day, when he handed me a card. I asked him what the gentleman said who left it. He replied, that he said he wanted to pay me something. 'But,' said I, 'he owes me nothing.' 'Well, that's what he said; but I can't remember what it was he wanted to pay.' 'Was it his *respects?*' said I. 'Oh! yes, sir,' he answered, evidently much relieved, 'that was it.'

I, for the first time, was reading 'Gil Blas': I had finished the first, and had begun the second volume. It was a dark, snowy day, and no visitors came in to interrupt us. The boy took up the first volume, as he sat on one side of the stove, and I on the other. As we read on, the humor of the book would prove too much for my risibles, and I would be forced to laugh aloud; then the boy would respond at something he had come across: so there we were, master and man, both enjoying the witty story with equal delight. I think if the author could have seen us, he would have laughed as heartily as either.

I had now become intimately acquainted with Mr. Allston. His habits were peculiar in many respects. He lived alone, dining at six o'clock, and sitting up far into the night. He breakfasted at eleven or twelve. He usually spent three or four evenings, or rather nights, at my house every week; and I greatly enjoyed his conversation, which was of the most polished and refined order, and always instructive. I sometimes called at his studio. It was an old barn, very large, and as cheerless as any anchorite could desire. He never had it swept, and the accumulation of the dust of many years was an inch deep. You could see a track, leading through it to some remote corner of the room, as plainly as in new-fallen snow. He saw few friends in his room;

lived almost in solitude, with only his own great thoughts to sustain him.

Just before I sailed for Europe, he had shown me his great picture of the 'Feast of Belshazzar.' It was then finished, with the exception of the figure of Daniel. I thought it a wonderful picture. I was not to speak of it to any one but Leslie. During the three years of my absence, he did not work on it. I had a fine, large studio; and, when I went to Washington, which I did in the winter of 1828, I gave it to Mr. Allston to finish his picture in. But he did not unroll it. He painted all winter, instead, on a landscape; and, when I came home, I found he had wiped out his winter's work, saying it was not worthy of him. He smoked incessantly, became nervous, and was haunted by fears that his great picture would not come up to the standard of his high reputation. One day, he went to his friend Loammi Baldwin, and said, 'I have to-day blotted out my four years' work on my "Handwriting on the Wall."'

He had discovered some little defect in the perspective, which could not be corrected without enlarging the figures in the foreground. Had he painted this picture in London, surrounded by the best works of art, and in daily intercourse with artists of his own standing, his picture would undoubtedly have taken a high rank among the best works of the old masters. As it is, it is only a monument of wasted genius of the highest order.

CHESTER HARDING

[The following letter from Washington Allston to Mr. Harding gives such an agreeable impression of the 'social nature' of the former, and at the same time pays so pleasant a tribute to the latter, that no apology is needed for inserting it.]

CAMBRIDGEPORT, MASS., *December 25,* 1838

DEAR HARDING — Your letter from Cincinnati brought me an unexpected pleasure (though some perhaps might not think so, from this tardy acknowledgement; but not *you*, who too well know that I am anything but a punctual correspondent), and I sincerely thank you for it. Independent of the satisfaction of being kindly remembered, it was a pleasure to me to hear of the success of one whom I so highly esteem. I regret, however, that this *sublime* place supplies too little subject-matter for a letter to enable me to make a proper return; and my visits to Boston are so rare that I can glean next to nothing from that quarter. I might indeed talk of myself; but that is a subject on which I seldom care to say much at any time. All I shall say on it at present is, that I have been, as usual, hard at work; to what effect, I hope you will see on your return. You know that I am never idle; and, if I bring but little to pass, it is because my notions of excellence are sometimes beyond my reach. I may add to this *indefiniteness,* that I expect to resume 'Belshazzar' in the spring.

You say that you think more of your art when you are away from home. This is natural, and must needs be so with one who has so large a family to care for. But I do not think it a subject of self-reproach that it is so; but there would be a just one, if you suffered even the love of art to supplant the duties you owe to them — I do not mean by the neglecting to provide for them, which would be unpardonable; but by taking the place of those personal attentions, those nameless kindnesses, that go to make up so large a portion of domestic happiness. I have often thought of your conduct with regard to your family, and always with increased respect. You have

144

Nathaniel Parker Willis

a good wife and good children; a fact that bears the strongest evidence of your right bearing as a husband and a father. Neither do I think that your attentions to them, liberal as I know them to be, have ever caused you to neglect your pencil. Your numerous pictures ought to set your heart at rest on that score. Upon the whole, I cannot but consider your lot a desirable one. Much as I love my art (and I believe no one ever rightly loved it more), I still hold it subordinate to my affections. But there is time for the exercise of both, except, perhaps, where grinding poverty allows no remission of labor. But, even then, no man who continues true to his social nature is ever without some redeeming moment, when he is at liberty to interchange kindnesses; and it is seldom that any one is ever wholly deprived of such moments excepting by his own fault. . . . Present my compliments to Miss Harding, who, I understand, is with you; and believe me, dear Harding,
Ever your faithful friend
WASHINGTON ALLSTON

At this period of my life, I became acquainted with N. P. Willis. He was the 'lion' of the town; was young, handsome, and wrote poetry divinely. He often met Allston at my house, and, I trust, recollects how swiftly the hours flew by. He is living, and it is not my province to speak of his fame. It is national, and will be cherished wherever the English language is read. The friendship then formed between us has never for a moment been disturbed.

During my stay in Washington, alluded to above, I painted many of the distinguished men of the day, such as Mr. Adams, Mr. Wirt, all the judges of the Supreme Court, etc. Among them was a full-length portrait of Judge Marshall, for the Athenæum. I consider it a good picture. I had great pleasure in painting *the whole* of such a man. I remember one or two little incidents connected with him, which amused me at the time. When I was ready to draw the figure into his picture, I asked him, in order to save time for him, to come to my room in the evening, as I could draw it just as well then as by daylight. He was glad to do so. An evening was appointed; but he could not come until after the 'consultation,' which lasts until about eight o'clock. It was a warm evening, and I was standing on my steps waiting for him, when he soon made his appearance; but, to my surprise, without a hat. I showed him into my studio, and stepped back to fasten the front door, where I encountered Mr. Storrs, M.C., and two or three other gentlemen, who knew the judge very well. They had seen him passing by their hotel in his hatless condition, and with long strides, as if in great haste; and had followed, curious to know the cause of such a strange appearance.

When I reëntered the studio, I inquired of the judge whether he did not come without a hat, and he said 'Yes'; that the consultation lasted longer than he expected, and he hurried off as quickly as possible to keep his appointment with me. When he was preparing to return to his lodgings, I urged him to take my hat; but he said, 'Oh, no! it is a warm night, I shall not need one.'

I again met Judge Marshall in Richmond, whither I went during the sitting of the Convention for amending the Constitution. He was a leading member of a quoit club, which I was invited to attend. The battleground was about a mile from the city in a beautiful grove. I went early, with a friend, just as the party were beginning to arrive. I watched for the coming of the old chief, He soon approached with his coat on his arm, and his hat in his hand, which he was using as a fan. He walked directly up to a large bowl of mint-julep, which had been prepared, and drank off a tumbler full of the liquid, smacked his lips, and then turned to the company, with a cheerful 'How are you, gentlemen?' He was looked upon as the best pitcher of the party, and could throw heavier quoits than any other member of the club. The game began with great animation. There were several ties; and, before long, I saw the great Chief Justice of the Supreme Court of the United States, down on his knees, measuring the contested distance with a straw, with as much earnestness as if it had been a point of law; and if he proved to be in the right, the woods would ring with his triumphant shout. What would the dignitaries of the highest court of England have thought, if they had been present?

I was again in Washington in the winter of 1830-31, when I painted the portrait of John C. Calhoun. During the sittings he invited me to come up to the Senate, as there was to be an interesting debate. Mr. Hayne was to speak on the subject of 'Foote's Resolutions,' in reply to a short speech of Mr. Webster. I accepted the invitation, and Mr. Calhoun admitted me as one of the many favored ones.

Mr. Hayne was most eloquent, and exceedingly bitter in his remarks upon Mr. Webster's speech; and so scathing in his denunciations of New England and her policy, that I felt his sarcasms were unanswerable. I think all the friends of Mr. Webster thought so too. The South side of the Senate were vociferous in their applause. At night, I went to see the fallen great man, as I considered him. My daughter was visiting Mr. Webster's daughter at the time. To my surprise, I found him cheerful, even playful. He had the two girls upon his knees. I told him I expected to find him in another room, pointing to his library. 'Time enough for that in the morning,' said he.

Mr. Calhoun gave me another sitting the next morning. He seemed to think the great champion of the North was annihilated. He said it was a pity he had laid himself open at so many points.

I needed no invitation to go to the Senate that morning. I went early to the gallery, and secured a seat among the reporters. As Mr. Webster entered the Senate, all eyes were turned upon him. He was elegantly dressed, and apparently less excited than any of his friends. I felt towards Mr. Webster as I imagine a criminal might feel who looks to his counsel to save him from punishment for some crime he is charged with. He soon, however, put me at my ease. As he proceeded

148

John Marshall, Chief Justice of the United States
Painted about 1830

with his speech, all his friends felt satisfied that victory was his. I asked Mr. Calhoun what he thought of Webster's reply. He said simply, but with great emphasis, 'Mr. Webster is a *strong man*, sir, a *very strong man*.'

'DEAR LYMAN — I am happy to reply to your kind favor of the 20th handed me by Colonel Dwight. It is a long time indeed, since any greetings have passed between us, though I do assure you that I have often in imagination been in Northampton. But I must not indulge in many preliminary remarks, or it will require more than one sheet to answer all your interrogatories. You probably know that I left Boston for Richmond with the intention of *taking off the heads* of the Convention. During my stay in that place, I painted eighteen portraits in all, and amongst them were the two vice-presidents, John Randolph and Chief Justice Marshall again. My visit, independent of any pecuniary consideration, was one that I shall long remember with pleasure. It was a noble sight to behold the first steps in the proceedings of that body. They, as you know, chose Mr. Monroe as the president. It was truly affecting to all present, when, after the unanimous voice of the Convention had proclaimed him their head, the Chief Justice and Mr. Madison led him to the chair. The stillness of death pervaded the whole house, which was only broken by the tremulous voice of the president.

149

Insignificant as this Convention was in comparison with that of Seventy-six, it nevertheless brought that illustrious body to my imagination very forcibly. Indeed, this trio of revolutionary veterans seemed almost a part of that august assemblage.

'I had frequent opportunities to hear the most interesting debates during my stay. I heard several of Randolph's happiest efforts, besides which I had the pleasure of seeing a good deal of the great luminaries in my own room.

'I had brought a letter to Randolph from General Hamilton of South Carolina, asking him to sit to me for his portrait. I presented it with considerable trepidation knowing something of his peculiarities, but my fears were groundless. I was most graciously received, and was assured that it would give him great pleasure to sit to me. At the close of the second sitting, he said, "If you have no objection to showing your sketch, I would like to see it. I know if it is like, it will be very ugly. Ah! it is *very* like."

'I painted four different pictures of Randolph during my stay, and I do assure you that I have never seen a more perfect gentleman in all respects, or a more entertaining or instructive companion than he was. His memory is stored with everything that can be called for by any occasion or any remark, no matter upon what subject, or in what strain.

'I was in Richmond about three months. I saw much

of the high life of the place. There is a great deal of broken-down aristocracy. Pride and poverty are singularly blended. Many an old family have lost the greater part of their estates, but still attempt the same style that they were wont to keep up when in the full tide of prosperity.

'Democracy is in its greatest force here, in one sense of the word. I do not wish to augur evil, but I venture the prediction, that Virginia has seen her manhood (forgive the Irishism) both morally and physically. You would be disgusted to see the low, bar-room dissipation that is spreading through all the younger part of society. No public spirit — no roads nor bridges, nor any public works, unless cock-pits and race-courses can be dignified by that name.

'Yes, my dear fellow, I did witness the late intellectual combats — at least so much of them as relates to Webster and Hayne. It was a glorious victory for New England. There was an unceasing hurrah of triumph by the Hayne-ites, after his first reply to Mr. Webster, and many of the friends of the latter feared the result, so good was his uncontradicted story. Indeed, the attack was in his most eloquent and biting manner. He closed his speech about three o'clock, the usual hour for adjourning, when Mr. Webster rose to reply, but some member moved an adjournment until Monday. From Friday till Monday there was nothing talked of, indoors or out, but Mr. Webster's set-down. Monday came, and at an early hour the Senate was filled to suffocation. Ladies and gentlemen were admitted to the floor of the Senate, ladies occupying the seats of Senators. The ordinary business of the morning was dispensed with, and Mr. Webster commenced speaking about 12.30 and spoke until half past four. The substance of what he said you have in the papers, and as you have heard him, you may imagine in part the effect. I never felt the power of eloquence before. I could not keep my seat. The "when, the how, the wherefore," is not done justice to in the report, nor can you conceive the effect the "Ghost of Banquo" had upon the audience. It is impossible for the pen to describe the interest that was kept on tiptoe from beginning to end. Not a man nor woman left the Senate until it adjourned.'

In the latter part of the summer of 1830, I had taken my family to Springfield, Massachusetts, to spend a portion of the warm weather. We were all so well pleased with the place that I exchanged my house on Beacon Street for one in Springfield, which has been our home ever since.

Little of interest occurred in my life for several years. Its monotony was varied only by several professional trips to the West and South.

In 1845 I met with a sore bereavement in the death of my wife. She died on the 27th of August, after an illness of but three days.

John Randolph
Painted about 1830

CHAPTER VII

At this point the story of Mr. Harding's life, as told by himself, ceases in any continuous form. The only indications of the course it followed for the sixteen years which intervened between the removal of his family to Springfield and his second trip to England are to be found in the few hastily written family letters which have been preserved, and from which the subjoined extracts have been made.

TO M. E. H.

'Boston, *June*, 1836

'I owe you *one* letter, and here you have it. You speak of several that I am indebted to you for. Now I deny the debt altogether. Every time I go home I consider the account settled, all debts paid; and when I leave, then a new one is opened. When I write to your mother I feel that I am writing to you all, and each one has the reading of my letters if they please, though I admit that some of them are so short that if they were to be divided amongst you all, the amount that each one would get would be small, as a pie before it is cut looks well, and to any one of the party would be a tremendous quantity, but apportionate it out in pieces and it is nothing at all. The sun, you know, can be looked at by millions, and none of its splendor be diminished.

Millions can receive warmth from it, and yet its heat be none the less. Just so it is with my letters: each one of the family can read and be edified and entertained by them without in the least decreasing their *value!* By this logic you will see that you are all largely my debtors. . . .

'You have heard of Dr. Stevenson's death. I feel his loss most deeply. He was an intimate friend as well as my physician. His is the first death that has occurred in our club since it was formed.'[1]

TO M. E. H.

'BALTIMORE, *October* 6, 1838

'Caroline wrote home yesterday, and I thought that would be the last you would hear from us, until we reached the great western valley. But as bad luck will have it we are detained one day more in consequence of the rascality of the stage agents. We leave here for Wheeling this afternoon, to sleep at Frederick, sixty-six miles from here; there we wait for the morning line until one o'clock to-morrow, and then we go night and day. What a prospect lies before us! Never mind, it will be all the same five hundred years hence.

[1] 'When I was a young man, and soon after Mr. Harding's return from his first visit to England, I belonged to a club with Harding, James K. Mills, Nat. P. Willis, Horace Mann, Dr. S. G. Howe, Charles Sumner, Edward G. Loring, etc., etc., who dined at each other's houses weekly and had grand good times, until some of our party became politicians, and the after-dinner talk on Anti-slavery became so personal that we had to break up the Club.' (Extract from letter of J. T. Reed to Samuel Bowles, of Springfield, Massachusetts.)

154

'It is as warm here as July — mosquitoes as thick as the flies in our kitchen. Caroline's face is much like the sides of a fine trout, full of red spots. In the trout this is a great beauty, but I very much question whether you would think said red spots any improvement to the face divine. I have no doubt it may be good for the health, as low bleeding is recommended for plethora.

'Last night closed the city election. It was a most violent contest. The result was known about midnight, and at one o'clock there came about forty drunken fellows into the hotel to greet one of the leaders. He was in bed on the same floor with us. I thought at first it was a company of dragoons. Caroline was in a room not far from me, and alone, though I thought Miss Shubrick was with her. She was almost frightened to death, so she said this morning. I should have gone to her rescue, only that I feared Miss S. might be as much frightened at me inside the room, as she was at the larks outside. . . .

'I hope you are improving your time by reading something useful. *Not a novel on any account.* Novels only weaken the mind and give a distaste for useful reading. "Johnson's Lives of the Poets" is a book I can recommend. But above all things whatever you read, do not forget.

'Aren't you astonished to see so scholar-like looking a letter from such a quarter? I hope you will make the proper acknowledgment of the same.'

155

CHESTER HARDING

TO J. M. K. [1]

'New Orleans, *January* 18, 1840

'We have had some extreme cold weather here. The other morning I thought I discovered some signs of white frost, although the mercury did not indicate so low a temperature. I presume there has been no doubt on that point in Alton. For the last two weeks we have had no occasion for a fire more than half the time, and some of the days we have had our windows up like midsummer.

'W—— writes me that the times are as hard as ever in Boston. What are we coming to? If government will pass an act prohibitory of all foreign goods, I don't care how soon they pass an act to put down credit of every sort, public and private, and let the expenses of the government be paid by direct tax.

'Speaking of the credit system, I think your State and citizens are likely to have enough of it. By the time Benton's hard currency is in full operation, one dollar will of necessity be worth as much as five or six at the present time. How will Illinois pay her interest on her foreign loans? I think she will take the "benefit of the act," and private debtors will do ditto.

'We have had great glorification in this city. The "Hero of two wars" has been down here, but it was, as the boys say, "no go." There was less enthusiasm shown

[1] Judge John M. Krum, of St. Louis, Missouri, who had recently married his second daughter.

than I ever saw evinced for any public man who made a show of himself; — no shouting and throwing up of caps, except by boys and "niggers." This is a solemn fact, and it struck deep in the old General's heart. He often expressed great disappointment. I was grieved to see it, for whatever I may think of *President* Jackson, I certainly think most highly of *General* Jackson. It was believed here that the old man came down to electioneer for his son and heir, Martin the First. Whatever the effect may be abroad, I really think he lost more than he gained in New Orleans.'

TO J. M. K.

'SPRINGFIELD, ARTIST'S RETREAT, *July* 11, 1840

'Here I am, seated in our parlor with the windows closed, to keep out the flies and heat. The mercury is pretty well up in the world, though by the aid of the trees in front, together with the cooling pattering of the fountain, we can keep tolerably cool. This place looks more like fairy-land than ever. It is a lovely spot beyond a question, and if I had a fortune to enable me to keep it up as I could wish, there is no spot I should like better for the summer months. . . .

'In politics we are "going it strong" on the right track. I hope to see a change in the administration. We have had enough of experiments for the last twelve years, and I think that any change from this government of office-holders will be for the better. This eternal war upon credit and the currency has ruined thousands. Nothing but a United States Bank will put us right again. I rather think that the town you are now living in, and yourself included of course, would be worth five times as much as you now are if old Jackson had remained quietly at the Hermitage for the last twelve years. I know the office-holders will move heaven and earth to keep their places, poor disinterested creatures! But enough of this.

'I think I shall be obliged to go and try to get a little food for my wife and children this afternoon. What a sacrifice I make to keep my family in fish! But as fish is considered more wholesome than flesh in hot weather, I am willing to make it.'

Mr. Harding let nothing interfere with his devotion to his family and to his profession. He was always greatly interested in current events and was a firm believer in the policies and principles of the Whig Party, in which party he believed all political wisdom was centered. He was an ardent admirer of Daniel Webster particularly. Between 1830 and the time of Mr. Webster's death in 1852, he painted from life about twenty portraits of him. When Edward Everett stood for reëlection for the governorship of Massachusetts in 1839, the Democratic candidate in opposition was Marcus Morton. On election day, Mr. Harding was indulging in his favorite recreation of

Daniel Webster

fishing and lost his vote which would have been cast for Governor Everett. After the returns were all in, it was found that Marcus Morton was successful by a majority of one vote. Had Mr. Harding voted, there would have been a tie which would have thrown the election into the Legislature, which body, undoubtedly, would have chosen Governor Everett. To the day of his death, Mr. Harding deeply regretted this fishing trip.

TO C. HARDING, JR.

'Boston, *November* 3, 1841

'... There is one thing that I wish to impress upon your mind as of the utmost importance, which is, that you improve every moment of your leisure in classical and belles-lettres acquirements. I do not mean by this that you should turn over the leaves of the books you read for the sake merely of reading any given set of works. Fix indelibly in your mind the contents of every book you read, as so much capital laid aside for future use. It is better to read a little, understandingly, than to hurry through whole libraries. Regard each book as a fountain, and never go to it without carrying away some of its useful store. Ask yourself this question every time you sit down to a book — What object have I in reading this work? The answer will be, to get new ideas. Of what advantage will those ideas be to you? should be another question. Certainly not for present use merely, but they are to be treasured in your memory,

159

to be drawn upon as occasion requires through life. Look at the very common evil of careless reading. For example, a man reads the Constitution of the United States in the too frequent, careless way. A week or a day after, he is with gentlemen who are discussing this same document, and gross blundering statements are made as to this or that power granted or withheld. Ten to one the man who has so recently read it cannot put them right on a single point. The reading took him twenty minutes. How much better for him had he taken as many hours or days, if by so doing he could comprehend and treasure up its contents.'

TO J. M. K.

'BOSTON, *November* 22, 1841

'. . . The next important matter to be communicated is the doings on account of the Prince de Joinville's ball, which comes off to-morrow night. Caro and I are all that are to go to the affair. Your mother, not having her dancing shoes in readiness, declines going, as she has a holy horror of wall-flowers. M., and W. too, decline. It is to be hoped that the Prince won't know that three out of my family stay away from the ball, as that circumstance would detract much from the compliment. Indeed, there is no telling what the effect might be upon the proud King of the French. The ball is to be held in the old Cradle of Liberty, and the supper is to be served in the large rotunda of

Quincy Market, the two being connected by a suspension bridge.'

'LEXINGTON, KY., *November* 14, 1842

'... I think it is quite doubtful whether I get as far as Cuba this winter. I really hope that I may find a fair demand for the commodity of heads in the towns on the Mississippi. Once I should have been delighted with the thought of a trip to a foreign country, but I begin to fear that I am older than I was twenty years ago. Perhaps the title [1] that you have helped me to has something to do with the idea. Whatever the cause, I have determined that this shall be my last trip from home.

'What a paradise this same Kentucky is! I'll venture to assert that the world can't produce a finer tract of land than is comprised in six or eight counties in this region. The good people lack nothing but the comforts of life. Luxuries they have in the greatest profusion, but in all the little trifles that go to make up the sum total of comfort, as we at the North understand it, they are wofully deficient. This may be a necessary concomitant of slavery. Perhaps it is wisely ordered; if the social system here were perfect, who would be content to toil out his existence in the sterile New England States?'

[1] Grandfather.

161

CHESTER HARDING

'SPRINGFIELD, *August* 14, 1842

'I have just returned from a trip to the White Hills, where I reveled in fine scenery, fine air, and magnificent trout brooks. When you feel like coming to this region, and wish to be born again physically, we will make up a party and spend a few weeks in that invigorating region. There is not another spot in this country where the weak can be made strong, the wretched made happy, and the poor made to feel rich. Therefore if you should ever be afflicted with any of these complaints, come on and be relieved.'

TO M. E. H.

'AUBURN, N.Y., SEWARD PALACE, *March* 10, 1843

'Here I am, ensconced in the gubernatorial chair, inditing a letter to my lovely daughter. But what shall I write? is the question that has just crossed my noddle. You know nobody here that I can speak of, and I know so few people that I could in any event have no gossip to relate. Here is the state's prison, it is true, but I have not been inside of its walls. It has a large family within, about eight hundred wretches who have violated the laws of the land, and are expiating their crimes.

'I'll give you a description of the family I am with. To begin with the head. A small man about the size of W—— D——; about thirty-five; aquiline nose; blue eyes; reddish-brown hair, and very agreeable manners.

162

William H. Seward

Madam is almost very beautiful; black eyes; dark hair; and a fine figure. She is very modest, and very intelligent; has read a great deal, and talks politics almost as well as her husband — not from choice, but only when others choose to give the conversation a political turn. She has the good taste to admire Mad. d'Arblay, and "The Neighbors."

'The Governor has resumed his practice at the bar as a lawyer. He spends his evenings at home in the library (which is very extensive), talking and smoking. I have now one of his cigars in my mouth, and a very good one it is. I wish I could send you one. But I will send you a kiss conveyed from my lips to the paper by the wet end of the weed. [Then follows a sketch of the lighted cigar.]

'I am getting on very well with my picture. I expect to complete my work here in all next week, when I shall set off for New York. . . .'

In the 'Life of William H. Seward,' written by his son, Frederick W. Seward, the statement is made that a fund was raised to secure a portrait of Governor Seward for the Executive Chamber at Albany, and that seven well-known portrait painters of the day were invited to visit the former Governor one after the other at his home in Auburn for the purpose of painting his portrait. All of these portraits were to be submitted to a committee, the one selected to be purchased and hung in the Executive Chamber. The committee decided that there were two portraits of equal merit, one by Chester Harding and one by Henry Inman, but, being unable to choose between them, it was decided finally to purchase both portraits and to hang one in the Executive Chamber at Albany and the other in the City Hall in New York. In Mr. Seward's book it is stated that the assignments were made by lot and that the Inman portrait was sent to Albany and the Harding portrait to New York, but this is probably an erroneous statement, for the full-length portrait of Governor Seward by Henry Inman is now hanging in the City Hall in New York.

CHAPTER VIII

In August, 1846, Mr. Harding made a second visit to England, where he spent nine months with profit and pleasure. During that time he kept no journal, other than the letters he wrote to his family, from which the following extracts have been made.

HALIFAX, *August* 18, 1846

We are thus far in safety, though not without peril. About eight o'clock of the evening of the first day, it came on very thick with fog, and we were booming along at a great rate through old ocean, when there came a sharp cry of 'Helm hard to port.' In less than half a minute we heard a most awful crash. We had run down a fishing schooner with eleven souls on board. The vessel sunk just at our stern, going under one of our paddle-boxes. Most of the men were below, and of course went down with the hapless craft. Five men were kept afloat until we lowered a boat and took them aboard. We were more than an hour in picking them up; we could hear their cries for help, but it was so dark that it was difficult to find them, and after they had been taken into the boat it took another hour for them to find the ship. We fired guns, but it seems they did not hear them owing to the noise of the waves, and but for the blue lights that were burned on board it is doubtful if they would have found the ship. The poor wretches were quite exhausted. We got calmed down again and were once more on our course, and I and most of the other passengers had turned in, when a similar cry of 'Hard to port' arose. All sprung up and rushed on deck, to see another schooner not twenty feet from us. Two minutes after there came another cry of 'Larboard *hard*,' and in like manner we just escaped a third smack. By this time there was very little disposition to turn in. The rest of the night we went at slow speed, and were right glad to see daylight. Two of the persons saved were brothers, one, a lad of twelve years; they lost their father and a brother. We raised a purse of $300 for the sufferers, giving $50 to the men saved and the rest to the relief of the widows of two of the men who were lost.

LONDON, *August* 30, 1846

Just at night of the fourth day from land, we fell in with some mountains of ice. Many of them were as large as the State House at Boston. One of them, the captain said, was two hundred feet high, and three times as broad at the base. It looked like a giant's snow-fort. While we were all admiring this sublime spectacle, the captain drew my attention to a small iceberg, nearly covered with water; telling me that it was those that were the terror of navigators. They are not easily seen in rough weather, and to encounter one would be as fatal as to run on to a reef of rocks. We made our port in eleven days and a half.

166

I find nobody in town that I want to see. I have strolled about a good deal, visiting my old haunts. Yesterday, I went to the National Gallery, and looked at the works of the old masters. Many of them I saw frequently when I was here before; but I find that most of them do not please me so much as they did formerly. I have dined with Pickersgill and Leslie, and visited their studios; but I am disappointed in the modern portraits that I have seen. I find, on looking at my own old pictures, that I was at least twenty years younger in the art than I am now, whatever I may be in years.

GLASGOW, *October* 11

Glasgow looks, in the main, just as it did twenty years ago, though it has spread out into the country, and has doubled its population. But it is sad to find my former friends grown so old. It is almost impossible to feel that these gray-headed men are the same persons that I knew so intimately when I was here before. I have looked in the glass to see if I can discover any change in my own looks; and sometimes I think I can discover a *slight* one.

October 12

The only thing in the way of my profession worth relating is that Mr. Alison, the historian, is sitting to me. What do you imagine he looks like? Of course you have pictured in your mind some image of the great author. He looks no more like one's imagination of an author

167

than I do like a bishop. He is nearly my own size, with a round, full face, of the complexion of Mr. Everett, reddish hair, large yellow whiskers; yet has rather a distinguished air. He is the sheriff of Glasgow, a very important office; and is highly esteemed by all classes.

The last ten days have been miserably dull and rainy. My only relief from the horrors has been in books. I have read Hazlitt's writings on art with a good deal of pleasure and instruction. I am now reading Alison's History. I commenced it, mainly, so that when he was sitting to me I need not have the mortification of saying I had not read his book. But since I have got fairly into the history, I have needed no such motive to induce me to go on with the work. It is beautifully written, and more exciting than any work of fiction. I am delighted with the 'Diary and Letters of Madame d'Arblay.' It is highly interesting. I would recommend it to your attention, if you have not already got hold of it. But don't let H. read it, nor any other book that does not directly or indirectly promote his studies. Light reading of any kind must dissipate the mind, and, at any age, make hard study uninteresting; but, to the *boy*, it is ruinous: of this I am well satisfied.

These same Scotch folks that I am among are a curious people. Close in their habits of economy, thrifty in business, always looking after their own interest, yet they are overflowing with hospitality. They always have some one or more to 'tak' pot-luck wi' them,' and

Sir Archibald Alison, the Historian
Painted in London, 1846

make dinner a social meal. They often sit two hours at the table; more for the sake of conversation than for drinking.

My habits are very regular. I rise at nine o'clock, order breakfast, smoke my cigar, and then go to work. I fast from that time until dinner, which is at six. I go home about eleven, and read till one; and then turn in to my bed. I am not sure but that I shall become a confirmed reader. I begin to feel great restlessness if I am idle a moment in my room.

November 1

Among my other pleasing occupations, I have had three or four of my teeth filled by the great dentist of the place. The reason I mention this circumstance is, that you may know the way I paid the bill. After he had finished the work, I took out my pocket-book, and asked him how much I had to pay. '*Nothing,*' said he; 'I never charge artists for any such small jobs.' Do you think Dr. Perkins would have so much consideration for the arts?

Yesterday, I dined again with Mr. Alison, and met Mr. Lockhart and his daughter. He is very agreeable and gentlemanly. His daughter is rather pretty, and simple in manners. After the ladies retired, Mr. Alison joined Mr. Lockhart and myself; and we were carrying on a very interesting conversation on the arts (here the arts are the subjects for general conversation, as much

169

as politics are with us), but, horrible to relate! just at this happy moment, I was attacked most violently with one of my turns of colic. I resorted to my usual remedies, but found little relief; and was obliged to get into Mr. Alison's carriage, and drive home. This is the first attack I have had for three or four years. I would rather have had it at any other time, as it deprived me of a most delightful party. I wanted much to have made some conversation with the grand-daughter of Sir Walter Scott. But, Pegos, what *is* is.

November 15

They have in this city just opened an exhibition on the plan of the Athenæum, only not equal to it in point of merit. I was invited to see it, the day before it was opened to the public. There are many pretty good pictures, but none first-rate. They are very proud of it; and one of the principal artists asked me, with apparent pride and exultation, if we had anything of the kind in America.

Nothing of any great interest has crossed my path since my last. I have had no great dinners, no colic; things have gone on very monotonously. The sun has not been seen for the last ten days, and fears are beginning to be felt for his safety. When last seen, he was struggling through a dense mass of smoke and fog.

Dear daughter, as the great day of all New England days approaches, I cannot but wish that I could form

Margaret E. Harding (afterwards Mrs. White)
The artist's daughter at the age of fifteen

one of the party around C.'s table. You may be assured
that I shall be in the midst of you, in spirit. This morning I was awakened by a friendly knock at my door. I
was dreaming at the time, most delightfully, of being at
home with Caro. and you and the C.'s; and it was painful to be so suddenly aroused to the reality of being in a
far-off land. I would not have you infer from this that I
am discontented or unhappy, for it is not so; and so long
as I receive letters regularly, assuring me that all is going on well with you, my dreams of home and friends,
whether in my sleeping or waking hours, will only in-
crease my happiness. So God bless you all!

November 25

I heard that the Duke of Hamilton was at his place,
about a dozen miles from here; so this morning I took
coach to go and see him; but, to my great disappointment, he was not at home. The palace is shown to
visitors on Tuesdays and Fridays; so, as this is Wednesday, I could not get in. I told the servant that I knew
the duke, and had painted a portrait of him. Still I could
not get the housekeeper to break over the law. I started
off, but had not got more than twenty rods, when a liv-
eried servant, without a hat, came running after me, saying that Lady Douglas, the duke's daughter, wished me
to come back, and see the palace. The housekeeper had
told her who I was. I spent an hour or two in looking at
the pictures. Some of them are very fine. There are

several Vandykes, and also the celebrated picture, by Rubens, of the Lion's Den. The gems in the way of furniture are most exquisite. The tables and cabinets, inlaid with gold and precious stones, are wonders in the mechanic arts.

The grounds are very extensive. From the front door of the palace you look down an avenue of trees about twenty rods in width and a mile in length, and perfectly level. The grass is as green as in midsummer. Then such ornamental gardens, and kept in such exquisite order! They even *surpass ours at home!* The house, too, is *considerably* larger than ours. It is about four times as large as the State House at Boston. We shall never see anything like it in our country. If one could step from this splendid pile into one of our fine houses in Boston, the contrast would be enough to curb the ambition of the proudest. The main part of this splendid building is not yet finished, though it was up to the first story when I was here twenty-two years ago, and the architect has been all the time at work upon it. Everything about it is of the most durable material.

The question naturally arises, whether the owners of this princely mansion are any happier than those who live in more humble dwellings. In this case, I believe many a man who lives in a 'ten-footer' is far happier than Hamilton with all his titles and wealth. He and the duchess live in different parts of the house, keep separate carriages, and never travel together. There is this com-

172

fort in their case, the house is large enough for twenty families to live in it, without elbowing each other.

December 8

Yesterday, I took the cars, and went out to Lord Belhaven's place to dine. His carriage was waiting for me. I found a brilliant party of ladies and gentlemen. The conversation at table was quiet and unambitious, and I at once felt entirely at home. After dinner, Lady Belhaven was entertaining me with some curiosities in the drawing-room, when she came across a book of pressed leaves from America, which, she said, was a present from Mr. Everett. She wished me to tell her if they were true to nature: the colors were so brilliant that she could hardly think they were. I not only assured her they were so, but, what was more, that some of them came from a tree on my own place. I recognized the peculiar coloring of the leaves on the maple by our gate, and remembered when L. was visiting you, and gathered them to send to her uncle.

LONDON, *January* 6, 1847

Presented my letter to Mr. Rogers.[1] He is an old man — I do not know how old, but I should think at least eighty. He stoops a good deal. He has a pale face, with fine head, and features full of expression. I hope he will sit to me for his portrait; but all these lions have been

[1] Samuel Rogers, the banker-poet.

painted so often, that I wonder how they can treat a painter with decent respect. One of the greatest objections I have to becoming a great man is the tax I should have to pay in time and patience to the painters and sculptors. So I believe, on the whole, I won't become great. If, however, I am ever doomed to that distinction, I will do my own painting. I think some of anticipating that event by beginning a portrait of myself at once, and sending it to the Athenæum. If I do commit such a folly, I intend to paint it in a choker and make it look as much like a gentleman as the case will admit of.

January 8

I breakfasted to-day with the author of 'Italy.' We sat down at breakfast at half past ten. We had good tea and coffee, eggs, and cold game, with a variety of cold breads. In short, poets, that is poet bankers, live very much like prose bodies, for aught I can see.

Mr. Rogers is most charming in conversation. He is familiar with every subject both in and out of letters. He admires Prescott very much, and thinks him one of the best writers in the English language. He thinks Mr. Webster one of the greatest men living, and idolizes Mr. Everett.

January 16

I have made a beginning of the portrait of Mr. Rogers. It is very troublesome, on account of his deafness, to keep him animated. Once, to-day, he fell asleep while sitting.

He remarked, in the course of conversation, upon the importance some painters attach to the high finish of their hands. He said they ought to be so disposed of as to attract no notice, for it is considered the height of ill-breeding to be found looking at a person's hands or dress in company. What would the good people of our country do, if they were deprived of the privilege of looking at the dresses, hands, and feet of the company they are in?

Mr. Rogers told me a story yesterday. He told it so well, that I am afraid to attempt to relate it; but I will try to give you the gist of it.

About forty years since, a clergyman in Scotland married a young and beautiful wife; and hardly was she his, when she died. He was overwhelmed with grief. The night after she was buried in the family tomb, he was sitting up late, and the waiting-maid was watching her almost distracted master, when he heard a knock at the door. He exclaimed with great agitation, 'That is Mary's knock!' It was repeated, and he again cried out that it was Mary's knock; and again a third time. But the maid would not go to the door. He at length opened it himself, and Mary fainted in his arms. The sexton violated the tomb; and, in attempting to wrench the wedding ring from her finger, he aroused her from her trance. The sexton fled; and she found her way home, and presented herself in her winding-sheet, a living ghost, to her husband.

CHESTER HARDING

Imagine Allston telling the story, and you will get a pretty good idea of Mr. Rogers's manner.

The times are very inauspicious for my work. Trade is dull; and the fear of distress in England makes men stare at each other, and wonder where it is to end. All one hears or reads in the papers is so full of the famishing Irish, that one almost wishes one's self in the blessed United States. The debates in Parliament, last night, give a gloomy picture of the present, and offer little hope for the future condition of that unhappy country. It was stated that one family subsisted, for several days, on a carrion carcass of a horse that was so far decomposed that the crows had left it. It seems that a great portion of the Irish ordinarily live on potatoes, at this season of the year; that resource failing, they have nothing to substitute for them, and have no money to buy anything to keep body and soul together. Only think of the coroner sitting on the dead bodies of twelve or fifteen in a day, in a small village, all of whom died of hunger! It is awful indeed.

February 25

I went to a small party last night, at Mr. Bancroft's. He had a dinner-party; and, when I arrived, the gentlemen were still at the table. I went in and took a seat, and listened to an animated conversation between a Captain Wormley and a Scotchman. There was something striking in the broad accent and the good sense of

176

the Scotchman, which attracted my attention. After listening a while, I inquired his name; and who do you think he was? No less a person than Thomas Carlyle. I was afterwards introduced to him, and had a good deal of conversation with him. He talks well, easily, and naturally, and without the least tincture of Carlyleism. He has a hard face, stiff hair, and, in short, is as unlike the literary dandy as any farmer in the land.

March 25

I am now just finishing the picture of Lord Aberdeen. I must here relate a little incident which is rather flattering to me. We — that is, my lord and I — were speaking of the Irish, the other day; and I remarked that the more that is given in charity, the more will be expected, and illustrated my views by a story, which was this: I was riding on top of a stagecoach, on Cape Cod, one cold February day, when I espied a flock of sheep in the field, trying hard to get something to eat from the frozen ground. I said to the stage-driver, 'Is it possible these sheep run out all winter?' 'Yes.' 'Of course they feed them?' 'No,' said he, 'they used to do so; but the farmers find when they feed them that they won't help themselves, but only hang about the pen and bleat all day. But, if they are left to take care of themselves, they manage to get a living, and come out very well in the spring.' The next time his lordship gave me a sitting, he said that he told my sheep story to Sir Rob-

177

ert Peel, at the Queen's table; and it struck him very forcibly.

To-day was Drawing-Room at the Palace of St. James. I did not go, because I was not 'expected.' I went, however, to see the pageant, but was just two minutes too late to see the Queen arrive. So I waited an hour and a half for her return. I took care to get a good stand, where I was not more than twenty feet from where she must pass; and then waited with the patience of a martyr. At last the royal procession started. All were on tip-toe. I was tall enough without that resort. She had come so near that I could just discern a face in the carriage, when, most provokingly, a life-guardsman rode alongside of the carriage, and interposed his huge body just between me and her Majesty, so that I only saw her nose. I did not think the sight of that feature worth the trouble I had taken; so I set it all down as a piece of mummery, and went with my friend to see the new Italian opera-house.

Mr. Rogers says the 'New Timon' is attributed to Bulwer. He does not seem to think so much of it as you Yankees do. He says Bryant or Longfellow are, either of them, very much before that author, whoever he may be. He often speaks of Bryant in very high terms, and thinks it is to be regretted that a man of such genius should waste his energies in editing a newspaper.

Chester H. Krum (afterwards Judge Krum),
Harding's First Grandson, as a Child

CHESTER HARDING

Glasgow, *April* 17, 1847

I left London on the 5th for this region. My friend C. advised me to come by steamer from Fleetwood. I dread the sea, particularly the Channel. However, the weather was promising, so I booked for Fleetwood. It is a run of twelve hours. We started at seven in the evening, and had a very quiet night. When we were within about an hour's sail of our port, there came a heavy shower of rain, accompanied with high wind. The sea was almost immediately thrown into a terrible commotion; so much so, that the captain thought it unsafe to go into port, where the water was shallow, at low tide. So we put off twelve miles to the island of Arran. The wind increased to a terrific gale. We dragged our anchor several times before we fairly got settled. A boat, with four men, came out from shore (where the water was quite smooth, being under cover of the mountain), making for the steamer; but, as she neared us, she got into the wind, and was blown out to sea at a fearful rate. The captain pulled up anchor, and went after them; and, with much difficulty, got the poor wretches on board. They were completely exhausted, and in a half-hour more would in all probability have gone to the bottom. Another two-masted, open fishing-boat dragged her anchor, and was driven out to sea; but, fortunately, a steamer was making for the port we lay in, and picked them up. We lay here until two o'clock; and then, as it was high tide, we put out for the port of our destination.

179

But I cannot describe to you the horrors of the scene: it was perfectly awful. The wind blew as if it would blow our steamer out of the water. The wind was partly on our side, which made the ship lurch frightfully. One wheel would be ten feet above the water, while the other would be entirely covered. But we had the most perilous part of our voyage still before us. The channel to the harbor is narrow, crooked, and rocky. I never saw such breakers! However, we escaped all the dangers; and I never was so glad to put myself on firm footing as when I stepped on shore. We had many ladies on board; all were sick and terrified. Most of the gentlemen were in the same plight. I was not sick; but I cannot say I was not frightened. Half the town were on the wharf to see us come in. We found the railway train waiting, and in an hour we were safe in Glasgow.

I remained in the city three days, and then set off for the city of the 'Fair Maid of Perth.' I spent four days there, and had two days of *salmon*-fishing. I do not know that I shall ever be able to bring myself down again to trout-fishing. But to the sport. We fitted up and went into the boat, and fished for an hour. We were beginning to think we should have no sport, when, all of a sudden, a salmon took my fly. Jehu! how I was excited! But I tried my best to keep cool, and finally succeeded in landing him. He weighed sixteen pounds. This was considered a great feat, as it is seldom a man lands his first fish. I took two more before night, and went home well satisfied. The next day we had no right to fish for salmon, so we took a tramp of ten miles, and fished for trout; but it seemed like child's play. The day after, we tried the salmon again, and I killed two more; which was doing more in two days than any sportsman has done in a fortnight. I am told by Mr. Stirling that I am talked of as much by the gentry for my exploits as old 'Rough and Ready'[1] is for his. But, above all, I am glad to find my health improving.

May 8

This is the last letter you will receive from me from London. I am booked for the 4th of June. I am sorry to return to the States without having seen more of the Old World; but my means will not allow of my making the grand tour. As I have told you, my health has been such that I have been able to paint but little for the last three months, and it is too enormously expensive to live in Europe without a pretty liberal income. I sometimes fear I shall have to give up painting altogether. I have great faith, however, in a little quiet living at home, with my chicks about me. My trouble is a tendency of blood to the head.

May 14

I went last night to see Jenny Lind. I saw her in my favorite opera of 'La Sonnambula.' She entirely came up to my *youthful imagination*. I had no conception be-

[1] Gen. Zachary Taylor.

fore of perfect music and acting combined, as one sees
them in this Swedish Nightingale. She acted the part of
Amina so perfectly, that it became reality. It is impossible that she did not feel the sentiments she uttered,
so completely would her countenance and complexion
change with the passions of grief or joy or rage; at times
being as pale as a ghost, and then fresh as a rose. Her
voice and execution are wonderful. I never saw an audience, not even at the Tremont Theatre when Mrs.
Wood was carrying everybody away, half so much excited. Bouquets of flowers were showered down on the
stage, with shouts and waving of handkerchiefs. When
she addressed herself to the flowers —

> 'Not thee — of dear affection —
> Are the sweet pledges,' etc.,

I thought we should all have gone mad. The Queen and
Prince Albert were there; but they attracted no attention.

During his stay in England, Mr. Harding made two
trips to Paris, mainly to visit the picture galleries. The
last one was upon the occasion of the great annual exhibition of modern pictures at the Louvre.

CHAPTER IX

MR. HARDING spent the winter of 1847–48, which followed his return from England, in Washington, and there enjoyed a renewal of his intimacy with Daniel Webster, with whom he and the Hon. George Ashmun, and one or two other gentlemen who 'messed' together, were in the habit of dining two or three times a week. He writes: 'These family dinners were charming. We always found sumptuous fare, though not elaborate. Often the great feature of the feast would be chowder or dunfish, in both of which dishes he excelled. . . . I had a few bottles of old Scotch whiskey, such as Wilson & Scott have immortalized under the name of "mountain dew." This beverage is always used with hot water and sugar. I put a bottle of this whiskey into my overcoat pocket, one day when I was going to dine with Mr. Webster: but I thought, before presenting it to him, I would see who was in the drawing-room. I put the bottle on the entry table, walked into the drawing-room; and, seeing none but the familiar party, said, "I have taken the liberty to bring a Scotch gentleman to partake of your hospitality to-day." "I am most happy, sir," was the reply. I walked back to the entry, and pointed to the bottle. "Oh!" said he, "that is the gentleman that bathes in hot water."'

Later, Mr. Harding says, 'I do think him the greatest man I ever came in contact with. He is not only full of wisdom and delightful anecdote, but of that sort of playful wit which startles the more, coming from the same fountain, as it does, with the wisest maxims that man ever uttered. With all this eulogium, he is far from being a perfect character. He lacks many of the essentials requisite in the formation of the good man. He lacks sympathy. He has the art of making many admirers, but few friends.'

It was during this winter that Mr. Harding painted the full-length portrait of Mr. Webster which hangs on the wall of the Athenæum; and also that of Henry Clay which hangs in the City Hall in Washington.

During a visit to Washington in the spring of 1844, Mr. Harding painted the portrait of Daniel Webster which now hangs in the lounge of the Algonquin Club in Boston. An interesting story is connected with this portrait, it being believed that possibly it saved Mr. Webster's life. It seems that the final sitting was to have been at ten o'clock on a certain morning, as Mr. Harding had arranged to leave Washington for Baltimore in the afternoon. Mr. Webster, who was at the time again a Senator from Massachusetts, but who had lately resigned his portfolio as Secretary of State in the Cabinet of President Tyler, sent word to the artist that the final sitting would have to be postponed for a day, as he had been invited to accompany the President and his

184

party on a trip down the river on the Princeton. Mr. Harding at once called on Mr. Webster and told him of his engagement in Baltimore and pointed out that he and others would be greatly inconvenienced if any change should be made in the date for the final sitting. The statesman thereupon wrote a note to the President declining his invitation and kept his appointment with the artist. The Princeton bore a distinguished company composed of the President, members of the Cabinet, and several Senators and Representatives. A large gun called the 'Peacemaker,' which was mounted on the deck, was fired several times, but unfortunately once too often. The gun burst, one fragment barely missing the President's head, while others struck the Secretary of State, Hon. Abel P. Upshur, and Senator Gardiner of New York, killing them instantly. Several others were injured. Had Mr. Webster been a member of the party, he, undoubtedly, would have been in the group near the gun and probably would have been killed or injured.

TO J. M. K.

WASHINGTON, January 23, 1848

. . . I suppose I am to paint Mr. Clay for the citizens of Washington, unless he refuses to sit. The subscription paper is circulating. He is averse to sitting, but he said in my presence, the other evening, that 'if the thing could not be stopped, he should have to sit.' I met him at a party at Mr. Bodisco's (the Russian am-

185

bassador), and it seems the mayor of the city had spoken to him about the picture. As I shook hands with him he said, 'I learned to-day, *with some apprehension*, that you were in town.' I can't blame him, for I don't know a greater bore than to sit for a portrait.

Washington is a very pleasant place for the winter, in many respects. One meets with the great men of the nation, and withal the climate is good. I dined yesterday with the Speaker, and met Governor Seward, Senator Rives of Virginia, and a dozen other lesser lights. Mr. Rives is full of brightness and perhaps talent, but it strikes me that Seward is the greater man of the two. Webster is head and shoulders above all the great men that I have met here. He has more wisdom and wit and everything that marks the great man than all of them put together. I can, however, hardly draw a just comparison between him and Mr. Clay, from my own observation, as I know so little of the latter. I have met Mr. Webster at small dinner and supper parties, and I must say that he never appears greater than when he throws off the great man. Mr. Calhoun called on me the other day, and sat and talked for an hour. He certainly talks well, but his talk in private is only a synopsis of his talk in public, all charming, but not so charming as Webster's volleys of wit and wisdom, which are always happily blended.

Henry Clay

CHESTER HARDING

TO M. E. H.

WASHINGTON, *May 3*, 1848

I left Baltimore last evening, and shall return this evening. My business here is to look after the pay for Mr. Clay's picture. I fear the 'look' will be comparatively fruitless. Many of the subscribers refuse to pay up, on the ground that by his last letter he has blasted his prospects for the nomination and election. . . .

I shall leave Baltimore in a few days for the North. Not that I have any designs upon the poor, unsuspecting trout, for I have a chance of doing a little in that way in this region. Yet I like the climate of the North, I like the people of the North, I like my home at the North, and I mean to go North very soon.

The winter of 1848–49 was spent in Buffalo. The following little incident, which occurred while there, amused Mr. Harding highly, and he thus relates it:

'I wrote to A. S. Upham, then senator from Genesee County; and directed the letter, as usual to *Hon.* A. S. Upham. Mr. Upham had been a wagon-maker; and was, like myself, a self-made man. He was at this time engaged very extensively in car-making for the New York Central Railroad. As I did not receive an answer as promptly as I expected, I wrote him another letter, and directed to *Mr.* A. S. Upham, *Wagon-maker*. This he answered at once, and directed the letter to Mr. Chester Harding, *Sign and Chair Painter*.'

187

CHESTER HARDING

Although Mr. Harding continued to follow his profession, during the winter months, even to the last year of his life, his active career as an artist began to decline from this time. He says of this period of his life:

'As I find myself growing old, and my family grown beyond my immediate care, I vary my pursuits. I always had a passion for field sports, and have, for the last twenty or thirty summers, indulged more or less in the pastimes of shooting and trout-fishing; and have found them healthful and innocent. I have spent many seasons among the White Hills; and, in later years, much of my summer leisure has been spent at the Saguenay, Lower Canada. This place is becoming a resort for excursionists. It is certainly a wonderful river, wonderful for its depth and bold shores, and the shoals of porpoises that are sporting in the tide. Hundreds of the white porpoise may be seen at almost any hour of the day. The scenery on this river is grand. A Church or Bierstadt might revel in it.

'I wish to record my appreciation of the hospitality I have received at the house of Mr. Radford, for six consecutive summers. He is the only Englishman living at the mouth of the Saguenay. He fills the several offices of magistrate, postmaster, and collector of the port. All the inhabitants of the neighborhood, with this exception, are of the lower order of the French. Trout-fishing is the principal amusement, with an occasional fight with the salmon. One meets many gentlemen sportsmen from Montreal and Quebec. Altogether, I think this place the most attractive, for the lovers of sport and grand scenery, of any resort I have ever visited.'

Mr. Harding spent his winters in some of the large cities, as Boston, New York, Washington, or St. Louis; but, though familiar with them all, none seemed to him so much like home, or claimed so large a share of his affections, as Boston. He says:

'I have been, from infancy, such a cosmopolite, that I can hardly claim any portion of the United States as home; yet I feel that I owe more to Boston than any other place; more of my professional life has been spent in that city than anywhere, and it is around it that my most grateful recollections cluster. The liberal patronage I have received, and the friendships I have formed there, make the place dear to me. The most liberal patronage I have enjoyed has been, perhaps, from the Lawrences. I have painted all of them, and many of their children. My full-length portrait of Amos Lawrence[1] I consider the best thing I have ever done in my whole artistic career. I also painted a full-length of Abbott Lawrence.

'I am proud to record my acknowledgment of many kind attentions from this noble race of men. Their character for enterprise and their success are not more

[1] Now in the home of Bishop William Lawrence at 122 Commonwealth Avenue, Boston.

189

remarkable than their noble bequests, as the institutions of the State can attest; while the poor of the city were not overlooked in their bounties. Few men leave a prouder record behind them.'

It has been impossible to procure very much information regarding the last fifteen years of Mr. Harding's life. The death of his wife in 1845 was a severe bereavement and, although at the time he was only fifty-three years of age, he never thought of another marriage. His home on Chestnut Street in Springfield, Massachusetts, is described in a book which was published many years ago by Mrs. Charlotte E. Warner, an aunt of General Clarence R. Edwards, entitled 'Chronicles of Ancient Chestnut Street.' This residential district, however, has long since disappeared. In his later years, Mr. Harding made his home with his daughter, Mrs. John L. King, of Springfield, for the greater part of the time, although his winters were usually spent in St. Louis at the home of his second daughter, Mrs. John M. Krum. His children are all dead as are many of his grandchildren, and the two surviving granddaughters who ever saw him remember him only as a kindly old gentleman, who spent part of his time in his studio and took many trips fishing for trout and salmon.

The latter years of Mr. Harding's life were overshadowed by anxieties growing out of the Civil War. He was the more oppressed by them, as he had four sons in the contest; two on each side. Scarcely any record

Amos Lawrence

of this period remains, however. The scanty extracts which are appended may give some slight indication of his views and feelings during the early part of the struggle. No one rejoiced more than he at the final cessation of hostilities.

TO HIS SON IN ALABAMA

NEW YORK HOTEL, *December* 21, 1860

It seems that the first step in the march of revolution was taken yesterday by South Carolina, and I fear other States will take the same insane course. Though there are many loud-mouthed demagogues at the North, there is yet a large majority in the free States who are willing to do justice to the South if they could be allowed time to act in their legislatures. All the obnoxious laws would be repealed, and I think the North would be willing to give any additional guarantees to the South for the fulfillment of their constitutional obligations. This rash step of South Carolina, however, closes the door against amicable adjustment of the troubles. What is to be the end of it is beyond the sagacity of man to foretell. We must wait the course of events with what patience we can. I fear the dream of peaceable secession will never be realized. Once let the mad spirit of revolution loose, and the most direful consequences are to be dreaded. Still I hope on, though it is hoping against hope.

CHESTER HARDING

TO J. M. K.

NEW YORK, *August*, 1861

Things look a little better in Missouri, when viewed from a distance; how long they may continue so remains to be seen. The enemy is very sharp and no one can guess their next move in your State.

The loss of Lyon was a serious one. We have not many such to spare. I do think that it was his own rashness that caused him to fall. There were probably twenty rifles levelled at him at once. Why should he have made himself so conspicuous a mark for the sharpshooters? Why not have the general in a less prominent place, with nothing to attract the fire of the enemy? . . .

I have just returned from Chateauguay Lake. All the way to this place I saw troops at the stations; some just recruiting, others on their way to join their regiment in Boston or New York. There will be no lack of men; the question then comes, have we enough of tried commanders? Of what use are the best of troops under incompetent leaders?

I expect to dine on Sunday next on a haunch of venison which I killed and sent home ten days ago.

TO W. O. W.

SPRINGFIELD, *December* 25, 1862

We hear from St. Louis often, but nothing from the soldier boys. It would be wonderful if we did not, before the strife is over, hear something of a painful character; but let us hope for the best. The news from the Western army is not very cheering, as I view it, and what has come to us from the Army of the Potomac is painful in the highest degree, and I fear is only a foreshadowing of what is to come. Look at a regiment of a thousand men marching in platoons through the street; — see what a show of numbers! Imagine ten times that number dead and dying on the battle-field, and one will realize the horrors of war. I am too deeply imbued with this sad subject to write upon any less exciting topic.

Gold, as you will see by the papers, is worth 59 per cent premium; in other words one dollar of currency is worth about forty cents. How much lower it will go, no one can tell.

TO M. E. W.

1864

I am getting too old to enjoy city life. I feel somewhat like the old woman who was complimented on her youthful appearance. 'Oh, la,' she said, 'I am only fit for the kingdom of heaven, and hardly that.'

The last winter of Mr. Harding's life was spent in St. Louis, with his children there. During the winter, he painted a nearly full-length portrait of Major-General Sherman; and the fidelity of the likeness and the composition and finish of the picture were pronounced equal to any he had ever painted at any period of his life. He greatly enjoyed the work himself, and derived great pleasure from his acquaintance with his illustrious countryman, of whom he thus speaks, in a letter to a friend in Canada:

'I am now painting General Sherman, the real hero of the great war that has ended. He is a sort of Wellington in his appearance, small of stature, but full of character, and every inch a soldier. He has good and elevated notions of things, not only military, but political. It is a pleasure to have such a man before me, where I can tell him to turn this way or that, and to come at my bidding.'

That the pleasure derived from this acquaintance was in some degree mutual may be seen from the following note, written upon receiving news of Mr. Harding's death:

St. Louis, Mo., *April* 3, 1866

Hon. J. M. Krum.

Dear Sir — I have learned, with pain and sorrow, the death of Chester Harding, artist. I shall always remember the many pleasant, quiet interviews with which I was so lately favored by him, while painting my portrait; and beg you will consider me as one of his best friends. . . .

I beg to assure you of my deep and heartfelt sympathy.
Your friend
W. T. Sherman
Major-General

In June, 1889, General Sherman presented the

194

diplomas to members of the graduating class of the United States Military Academy at West Point. Brigadier-General Chester Harding, U.S.A., Retired, was a member of this class, and when he moved forward to receive his diploma, General Sherman, struck by the name, inquired as to his relationship to the artist. Nearly a quarter of a century had elapsed since General Sherman had sat for the portrait, and this incident evidences the favorable impression made upon him by the artist.

Mr. Harding left St. Louis, in the month of February, for his home in Springfield; but the journey proved a very severe one, and undoubtedly made a serious draught upon the strength of a man of his years. He thus describes it in a letter to one of his children:

SPRINGFIELD, *February* 27, 1866

DEAR M. — I am once more at home, after the worst time mortal ever had on the journey. I was snow-bound five days, during the coldest weather I ever saw, and in the poorest house that mortal ever slept in; no fire in my room, and none in the halls, with windows that let the snow drift in. I could only keep from freezing by piling on blankets, my own shawl, and overcoat; and then I could not have my hand exposed outside of the covering; it would have frozen in twenty minutes. I covered myself entirely, and drew myself up, much as you can imagine a bear to do when he is burrowing in midwinter. However, I am now all right. . . . I have a capital likeness of General Sherman, which he sat for in St. Louis. I think you would say at once that it is a capital likeness, without ever having seen the original.

After his return to Springfield, he occupied himself with putting the last touches to his picture of Sherman. Had he known it was to be the last work of his hands, he could not have labored on it with more care, or looked upon it with more affection. The pleasure and interest with which he used to pursue his work, in his younger days, seemed to have been aroused once more, as if to vindicate the undying nature of those qualities of mind and heart which constitute the artist. He put the finishing touch to the picture, the day before he started on his last journey to Boston. Some friend coming in, he playfully pointed out to him a stream of water he had introduced into the background of the picture, saying, 'That is a trout-brook; and there,' indicating the place with his brush, 'is the hole where the big fellows lie.' 'You ought to paint yourself there fishing,' responded the friend. 'No, indeed,' he replied; 'it wouldn't do for a little fisherman to stand by the side of such a big general.'

The date of the following note shows that one of the last acts of his life was a kindly one. It was from a brother artist who was struggling with ill-health and straitened circumstances.

196

General W. T. Sherman

CHESTER HARDING

DEAR MR. HARDING — My heart is too full for words. I cannot express my thanks for the very generous gift received from you yesterday. The least I can say is, I thank you most sincerely, and shall ever cherish the memory of one, who alone can possess so generous a heart to prompt to noble deeds. May the blessing of the Lord that maketh rich be yours!

Sincerely yours

———— ————

On March 27 he started for Boston, on his way to Sandwich, on Cape Cod, which was his favorite resort for trout-fishing in the early spring. He was, apparently, in good health and in fine spirits. On his way to the station, he met a friend, and, shaking his rod at him, called out, 'Never felt more like it in my life.' He took a severe cold on the journey and did not leave Boston the next day, as he had expected, although he was able to go to his club in the evening. His cold increasing, he was persuaded to send for a physician; but no alarm was felt, either by himself or his attendants, with regard to his illness. When asked if some of his family had not better be notified of his illness, he said, 'Oh! no; it is not worth while.' He was not confined to his room until Sunday morning; when, after getting up and dressing himself, a prostration so sudden and complete came over him as to make it a matter of great difficulty to get him onto his bed. From this time he sank rapidly. His mind seemed to sympathize with the weakness of his body; and he made no effort at con-

197

versation, and made no sign of having any consciousness of his situation. He breathed his last, April 1, at ten o'clock, Sunday evening, before any of his children, who had been summoned at the appearance of danger, could reach him. His death was such as he had often hoped for, sudden, painless, and before the failure of physical or mental powers.

His remains were taken to Springfield, and placed by the side of his faithful and beloved wife, in the cemetery which he had done much to adorn; and where he had seen gathered, one by one, most of that generation whose intellectual and social gifts and friendship for himself had made the place so attractive to him, when, thirty-six years before, he had selected it for his home.

His decease was announced to the public by the following appreciative notice in the 'Evening Transcript' of April 2, 1866:

We deeply regret to announce the death, at the age of seventy-three, of Chester Harding, the most venerable of American artists, and one of the most eminent and accomplished. He died last evening at his rooms in the Tremont House. Few persons in the country were so widely known, and so generally esteemed. A self-educated artist, who rose from the humblest beginnings to be the companion, as well as painter, of nobles and statesmen, he had that innate gentlemanliness which placed him on an equality with every circle in which he moved, while he never lost, in conventional society, the vigorous manhood which he had learned in the woods and fields.

It was impossible to see him without both liking and admiring him; he had in his heart, as well as in his manners, that quality which wins affection at the same time it inspires respect; and his constant regard for the rights and feelings of others was his shield against any invasion of his own. A duke who met him in a drawing-room, a country lad who was his companion in a fishing excursion, would find that his manhood was broad enough for both. He visited England twice; and there was hardly a place in the United States where he was not known. His conversation was rich in recollections of eminent men of all kinds in both hemispheres, while it was absolutely untainted by self-assertion and self-conceit. At one time we heard of him as painting Daniel Webster at Washington; and, soon after, that he had started off to the wilds of the West to paint Daniel Boone. One of his last works was an admirable portrait of General Sherman, which many of our readers will remember as among the finest things in the exhibition at the recent artists' reception. He had an instinctive attraction for all manhood, no matter what might be the field in which it was exercised.

The summers of his later years having been spent in many field exercises and sports, his old age was so hale and vigorous, that the announcement of his death will strike his friends with surprise as well as pain. Few men could leave behind them a more genial memory, or one which will be more warmly cherished by a large circle of friends.

One who had known him familiarly for a few years preceding his death thus writes:

Mr. Harding won upon my heart, as I believe he did that of every one, from the first; and he had that rare charm of manner which, while thoroughly dignified, made every one feel at ease; there was no false pretension or hauteur about him. His conversation was always rich and instructive; and, when with him, I invariably heard something which I should have been sorry not to know.

Moving, as he had familiarly, in the highest circles of rank and talent, he was singularly modest; and he seldom mentioned the distinguished people he had known, unless directly asked about them. He never coupled a duke and a dinner, nor prefaced a story with, 'When I was abroad with the Princess Orbitella.' ...

His host of friends will bear a life-long testimony to his virtues and accomplishments. These attributes

'Shall long keep his memory green in our souls.'

while his many masterly portraits will perpetuate his name in American art.

The late Chester Harding was not only a finished artist, himself, but did much to aid and encourage others to perfect themselves in drawing and painting. In 1841–1842, when in Boston, he gave much encouragement to the formation of 'The Artists' Association,' which, for the time, created much interest, and drew together a number of the then most successful as well as many of the young aspiring artists, who had not arrived at distinction in their profession. Allston was the acknowledged head, and Harding came next in grade.

Harding's gallery in School Street at that time became a popular place of artistic resort; and many will remember it as the scene of the revival of the arts in Boston.

Harding was very fond of trouting, and generally visited the White Mountains once a year, usually taking the stage to Conway and fishing up the Saco to the elder Crawford's, where he rested a day or two, and then branched off upon collateral streams, bringing home a well-filled basket of trout each night for a week. Sometimes he went to the Cape with like success, and would walk twenty miles a day to skim the brooks of their speckled tribe. Sometimes he wore high rubber boots, but generally waded in old leathers, with feet soaking ten hours at a time. — 'Springfield Republican.'

He had rare gifts of conversation, he attached his friends to him most warmly, he had a spirit of insight for discovering character, and an appreciative sense of the true, the beautiful, and the good. He was the Daniel Webster of his art, with like massiveness and compass of nature. — 'Boston Transcript.'

N. P. Willis, in 'The Home Journal,' thus alludes to the impression Mr. Harding made during his first visit to England:

Years afterward, I became a guest at Gordon Castle; and there, strangely enough, my best authority with the Duchess of Gordon, and the brilliant ladies who formed the court around her, was my assured intimacy with Harding the artist. Her ladyship's first question was of the 'prairie nobleman,' as they described this Western artist; and whom they considered a splendid specimen of a most gifted man, the American chance visitor to their titled circle, and the painter of some of their most distinguished portraits, a few years before. Visitor as I was on that same visit to Scotland, at Dalhousie Castle, I found my introduction everywhere the best, as the 'young friend of Harding the Artist.'

Harding's portraits, painted during his first visit to England, are all memorable. They have been treasured, I believe, as masterpieces, both of drawing and color, while the conceptions of character have been considered so felicitous as to be copied for reproduction in this country.

I shall give to our readers a treasure, if I transcribe a copy of an autograph letter from Harding, as it spreads open before me at this moment, describing one of these:

'September 2

'DEAR WILLIS — I have a portrait of the Duke of Hamilton which I wish to present to you. I should like to have it hang in your library. There is nothing in particular, of a historic character, attached to the original. But the fact that I painted it at a time in my life when my enthusiasm and ambition in art were at their highest, and it being the crowning point of my success as an artist in England, I hope will give it some value in your estimation. It gave me more applause, both in Edinburgh and London, than any picture I ever painted. It was exhibited in Edinburgh, and at the Royal Academy in London, and very flattering notice of it was taken in both cities. I have never been more fortunate in the coloring of a head, nor do I now think of any contemporary artist who has much surpassed it. Don't set this down as vanity. I can look at it as I would at any other *antique* — and my ambition is that it may be placed where it will be appreciated.

'With kindly regards to your lovely wife and children, I am your friend

'CHESTER HARDING'

The 'Boston Post' said of him:

He ranked with the representative painters of America and in him American art was made honorable at home and respectable abroad. When most who are now turned of ripe age were children, Harding was engaged in painting on durable canvas hosts of private men of worth, and an illustrious band of the public men associated in public life at Washington and elsewhere. If from the artist we turn to the man, we shall find enough to justify abundantly the strong hold he had upon private affection and individual esteem. He was a man every way free of reproach, and in all respects entitled to esteem, and fitted to inspire love. He was the father of a numerous family, now grown to manhood and womanhood, and settled successfully in various parts of the country. To them this blow will come with stunning effect. But his title to love and veneration were not limited to his relatives and his family. All who knew him loved him. He was of kindly, social feeling, and, for one of his years, convivial and jovial. He was ever young in his feelings and fresh in his views, and liberal in his opinions. Age rested gracefully upon him. His flowing white locks added a venerable aspect to his portly and commanding presence. He was not a professed scholar, nor a great reader beyond his art, or even in that; for he believed in the inspiration of artistic genius, rather than the studies of the closet. Although master of the great principles of his art, he needed only the human face divine and the pencil of his own genius to give life to the moving canvas. Hence he belonged to the order of original artists. He copied no man, and he flattered no man. He aimed in his art to be truthful, accurate, and just, hence he did not always please the vain nor satisfy the proud. A younger order of artists also were accustomed to complain that he fell behind the progress of art rather than kept pace with it. The modern innovations of mechanical painting of the human face, also, served somewhat to interfere with his eminence in the later years of his life. These annoyances from time and progress he bore with the spirit of a true artist. He knew that his fame was embodied in durable material, and that time, which interfered for the moment with his revenues and his popularity, would do justice to the great productions of his pencil. He knew that canvas, if less durable than bronze or marble, has somewhat of a hold upon immortality and will reach the judgment of posterity.

The 'Springfield Republican' says:

As a portrait-painter, he was one of the first in point of excellence that America has ever produced; and, in his time, he was the first, without dispute. . . . Nor had age dimmed his power, though it had tempered his ambition, and checked his industry; he, only last week, gave the finishing touches to a remarkable likeness of General Sherman, which he began in St. Louis, during the past season, from pure enthusiasm for the soldier and the man. It is among the finest of his works, and can hardly be excelled by any other likeness for spirit and fidelity. . . . Springfield knew him longest, loved him best; and she is proud that, since death must come to him, his ashes are to repose in her bosom.

At a meeting of the artists of Boston, to take notice of the death of Chester Harding, the following resolutions were unanimously adopted:

Resolved, That we lament the loss of our brother artist,

CHESTER HARDING

Chester Harding, who, for more than thirty years, has been to the elder of us a genial companion, and noble and generous rival; to the younger, a sympathizing friend and a worthy example, to the community in which he lived, an esteemed citizen; an exemplary husband and father, who has furnished to posterity, by his graphic and prolific pencil, representations of men of the day, and illustrations of contemporary history, which only posterity can properly value, but which have already placed him high in the ranks of American art.

Resolved, That we shall cherish the memory of his manly presence, and his generous and estimable qualities of head and heart.